# Biblical Texts and the Women Living with HIV and AIDS

**Biblical Hermeneutics Rediscovered**

The Series as the name suggests will focus on Biblical Hermeneutics, i.e., literary works concerned with methods of interpreting the Old and New Testaments of Bible via different stream of topics like Literature & Poetry, Indigenous Philosophizing, Ethical response towards Ecology, Health & Healing, Science & Technology, Feminist Theology, Sociological approach towards Human Rights, Law & Politics, Arts, History of Ideas, Ancient Civilizations, Cultural Contiguity, Religious Cosmologies & Mysticism, Appraisal of various Theologians, World Peace & Harmony, Global Capitalism, Network Marketing, Cybertheology, Population & Demographics, Epigraphic Studies, Contextualized Education, and many others. We welcome a Mss. on any topic/s mentioned, whether they are original works, scholarly monographs, collections of conference papers, revised dissertations, or translations of historical documents. Through the Series we, the Publishers, are striving to put forward published works that may help Institutions, Academic Bodies, Researchers, Scholars and the World at large in furthering their respective knowledge and understanding on the concerned subject. We welcome your comments on our efforts and further suggestions on how we can enshrine new ray of analysing & explaining the written Texts through our upcoming books.

*Biblical Hermeneutics Rediscovered - 16*

# Biblical Texts and the Women Living with HIV and AIDS

## Transforming Attitudes within the Indian Church and Community alongside the Medico-Legal Exposure

**T. Aaron Martin**

First Published in 2018 by

**Christian World Imprints**™
*Christian Publishing & Books from India*
H-12 Bali Nagar, **New Delhi-110015**
info@christianworldimprints.com
www.ChristianWorldImprints.com
Phone: +91 11 25465925

ISBN: 978-93-5148-286-4 (HB) ISBN: 978-93-5148-287-1 (PB)

**Cataloging in Publication Data--DK**
Courtesy: D.K. Agencies (P) Ltd. <docinfo@dkagencies.com>

**Martin, T. Aaron,** 1984- **author.**
Biblical texts and the women living with HIV and AIDS : transforming attitudes within the Indian Church and community alongside the medico-legal exposure / T. Aaron Martin.
pages cm. -- (Biblical hermeneutics rediscovered ; 16)
Includes bibliographical references.
ISBN 9789351482864 (HB)
ISBN 9789351482871 (PB)

1. HIV-positive women--India. 2. AIDS (Disease) in women--India. 3. Church work with the sick--India. 4. Church work with women--India. 5. Bible. Old Testament.--Criticism, interpretation, etc. 6. HIV-positive women--Legal status, laws, etc.--India. I. Title. II. Series: Biblical hermeneutics rediscovered ; 16.

LCC BV4460.7.M37 2018 | DDC 261.832196979200954 23



Printed in India.

This book in its original form is the thesis submitted to the Senate of Serampore College, towards the M.Th degree and is published with written permission. The author is responsible for the title, contents and opinions expressed in it.

**Dedicated to**

The Most Rev. Dr. M. Ezra Sargunam

Father Bishop of Evangelical Church of India

in commemoration of his $80^{th}$ birthday (July 19, 2018)

# Contents

# Acknowledgment

Brining out my presentation in the present book - form involved lots of care, concern and passion towards the targeted group in my network.

I am truly indebted to a number of individuals who have made the completion of this work possible. I would like to thank Senate of Serampore Registrar Dr. Santanu K. Patro for granting me approval for publishing my M.Th thesis. I am grateful to Rev. Dr. Monica Melanchthon for her careful, tireless, thorough guidance, and proof-reading. I also express my warm appreciation to Christian World Imprints for their initiative in publishing my writing. I am greatly indebted to ECI and MTSC family for their continued prayers and constant support. In particular, I acknowledge Bishop Ezra Sargunam, Bishop Sundar Singh, Bishop Rajasingh, Rev. Mrs. Kathiroli Manickam, Rev. Dr. David Onesimu and Rev. Duraiswamy for their persistent encouragement. Most of all, I want to thank my wife Evelyn and my father Rev. A. Thomas for their loving presence and faithful provision. Ultimately, I want to thank God for being my greatest inspiration and enabling me to accomplish something for God and people.

# List of Acronyms

| | | |
|---|---|---|
| AIDS | – | Acquired Immuno-Deficiency Syndrome |
| AWA | – | Ancient West Asia |
| AZT | – | Azidothymidine |
| B.C.E. | – | Before Common Era |
| BDB | – | Brown Driver Briggs (Hebrew and English Lexicon) |
| *CBC* | – | *Cambridge Bible Commentary* |
| cf. | – | Confer |
| e.g. | – | Example |
| ed., eds. | – | editor, editors, edition, editions |
| f., ff. | – | and the following pages |
| HIV | – | Human Immuno-deficiency Virus |
| IDU | – | Intravenous Drug Users |
| *JBC* | – | *Jerome Bible Commentary* |
| *JSOT* | – | *Journal for the study of the Old Testament* |
| MSS | – | Manuscripts |
| MT | – | Masoretic Text |
| MTCT | – | Mother-to-Child Transmission |
| NACO | – | National AIDS Control Organisation |

| | | |
|---|---|---|
| NGO | – | Non Governmental Organisations |
| *NIB* | – | *The New Interpreters Bible* |
| *NICOT* | – | *New International Commentary on Old Testament* |
| NNRTI | – | Non-Nucleoside Reverse Transcriptase Inhibitor |
| PMS | – | Pre Menstrual Syndrome |
| UNAIDS | – | Joint United Nations Programme on HIV and AIDS |
| Vol. | – | Volume |
| *WBC* | – | *Word Biblical Commentary* |
| WHO | – | World Health Organization |

# Introduction

HIV and AIDS pandemic has become a universal cancer by threatening the life sustainability of humanity. HIV and AIDS offer the greatest challenge to humankind in the form of widespread stigma, rejection, and discrimination due to fear, judgmental attitudes, etc. The impact of HIV and AIDS warrants a pedagogical response in biblical studies. Its incurability leads to fear, hopelessness, intense search for healing, poverty, death, orphans, widows, and overburdened families who have to take care of orphaned children. It underlines the need for transformative compassion.

In the Bible, there is no mention about the pandemic HIV and AIDS. But a similar outcome of the illness is recorded in the Biblical texts. The Bible is a source of authority which could be used as a tool to change the attitudes of an individual. In this research project, Biblical texts are looked at from the perspective of women living with HIV and AIDS, because they are doubly oppressed and are more vulnerable to this epidemic. In many cases, the Bible has been used to reinforce the discrimination and the stigma of the women living with HIV and AIDS. But, the Bible should no more be employed to subjugate sufferers, but its liberative elements need to be kindled for the welfare of the many sufferers. This is made possible by utilizing the "Reader Response Methodology". This postmodern approach accepts the reader to be an important contributor to the meaning of the text.

Three biblical texts from the Old Testament, namely, Numbers 12.10-16, 2 Kings 5:8 – 14, Ezekiel 37:1 – 14 are read from the perspective of women living with HIV and AIDS. In the first text, as per the traditional understandings, Miriam is blamed. But through readers' response method the blame is unmasked and the concern which she had about the life and witness of Moses is revealed. She is also called as a leader and there were also other seventy leaders upon whom the spirit of God descended. This story condemns the act of branding women living with HIV and AIDS as sinners. There cannot be any blaming of the women living with HIV and AIDS for their suffering. The act of excommunicating women living with HIV and AIDS invites critique citing Miriam's experience. In the second text, Naaman's skin ailment invites the readers to look the suffering underwent by him. Exposition of Physical, psychological, social and religious imaginations and sufferings of Naaman, gives the message of courage to women living with HIV and AIDS. In the third text, dry bones are brought to life using the words of the prophet Ezekiel. The message and the act of hope is delivered in the midst of a hopeless and helpless situation. This passage also gives a practical implication that since God is a God of life, women living with HIV and AIDS need not be rejected, rather accepted in the family and society with love, care and compassion. It motivates the suffering community to have an alternative consciousness which could affirm the very meaning and purpose of life.

This research stands as evidence that Bible stories about sicknesses could be re-interpreted from the perspective of women living with HIV and AIDS in order to provide quality care and to eliminate stigma and discrimination. This also becomes an agent of hope and words of encouragement in the midst of suffering. The reading proposed by the author calls the attention of the church and church leaders to encourage the faith communities to read the scripture from the perspective of suffering communities. When these stories of suffering are read with heart and mind, it gives space to relate oneself with the sufferers which might give some kind of consolation to the readers. It is also hoped that a biblical perspective on the issue would transform attitudes towards the HIV sufferer, which is so urgently needed within the Indian Church.

## Chapter 1

# HIV and AIDS

### Introduction

Aids is an ailment which does not allow the human immune system to function properly. This is caused by the virus called Human Immunodeficiency Virus (HIV). This virus reduces the efficiency of the immune system and leaves individuals vulnerable to many sicknesses. HIV is transmitted through direct contact of a mucous membrane or the bloodstream with a bodily fluid containing HIV, such as blood, semen, vaginal fluid and breast milk. This transmission is engaged through anal, vaginal or oral sex, blood transfusion, contaminated needles, exchange between mother and baby during pregnancy, childbirth or breastfeeding.

The HIV pandemic remains as the most serious infectious disease challenging public health today. HIV and AIDS affects different spheres of life like, cultural, spiritual, economical, political, social and psychological.

- Socially, it affects relationships at all levels

- Politically, it calls for particular kind of leadership at community, national and international levels
- Spiritually, due to its incurability several questions has been raised like, Does God care? Does God hear prayers or heal? Is God punishing us?[1]

## 1. AIDS – The Epidemic

AIDS a pandemic is an epidemic that spreads internationally and affects the entire globe. One may look perfectly healthy and still have HIV in their body. In fact, most people who are HIV positive do not yet have symptoms of AIDS. They grow to be completely sick due to exhaust of immune system. It is named as "opportunistic infections." A person can be HIV positive for months or years before being so damaged by the virus. After which the individual becomes defenseless to a variety of life-threatening infections. The origin of HIV and AIDS is not known or proven. It was unknown until the 1980s.[2] There are several theories, myths, and misunderstandings. Some may have heard and wondered: Did HIV virus transmuted from monkeys? Is HIV and AIDS a form of biological warfare? Is it a punishment from God for sexual promiscuity?[3]

## 2. How is HIV Transmitted?

HIV is found in blood, sex fluids of men (semen), sex fluids of women (vaginal fluid) and breast milk.

### 2.1. *Sexual Transmission*

Sexual transmission occurs with the contact between sexual secretions of one person with the rectal, genital or oral mucous membranes of another. Unprotected sexual acts are riskier for the receptive partner than for the inceptive partner. However, oral sex is not entirely safe, as HIV can be transmitted through both inceptive and receptive

1 Savitri Ramaiah, *HIV and AIDS* (New Delhi: Sterling Publishers, 2008), 11.

2 But it may have existed for many years before.

3 Facilitator's Guide, *Prescriptions for Hope* (USA: Samaritan's Purse, 2005), 15-19.

oral sex. Sexual Transmission is the major prevailing mode of HIV transmission.

### 2.2. *Exposure to blood-borne pathogens*

HIV can be transmitted through infected needles and contaminated blood transfusions. Sharing and reusing syringes contaminated with HIV-infected blood represents a major risk for infection with HIV. Blood transfusions are safe in hospitals and clinics where blood has been screened for HIV and where clean needles are utilized. Hospitals with best technology mostly will not have blood with HIV.

### 2.3. *Mother-to-Child Transmission (MTCT)*

The transmission of the virus from the mother to the child can occur during three stages:

*During Pregnancy:* This usually happens only when mothers are very sick and their placentas have broken down so that their fluids enter the womb and infect the baby. *During Labour:* A baby's skin is soft and sensitive. If the babies skin tears during labour, the mother's fluids can enter through the open tears.

*During Breastfeeding:* Breast milk is a fluid that could contain HIV.[4]

## 3. Misconceptions

There are several misconceptions about HIV and AIDS. Some of the most common misconceptions are:

- Sexual intercourse with a virgin would bring healing to AIDS
- HIV can infect only drug users and homosexuals
- Anal intercourse between gay men may cause to AIDS infection
- Open discussion about homosexuality and HIV in schools may become cause for homosexuality and AIDS[5]

---

4 Gracious Thomas, *AIDS in India* (New Delhi: Rawat Publications, 1994), 67-84.

5 Sanjiv Kumar, "Women and AIDS" in Women's Link, Vol. 2, No. 4, (1996), 11.

### 3.1. *Sexual Myths about Men*

A myth is a false belief that is defended as truth. Following are some of the sexual myth and myths about HIV and AIDS that exist among communities:

- The purpose of sex is to provide pleasure to the man only
- Getting married will take care of problems of lust and temptation
- Women are there only to serve, to be housewives and to have children[6]
- The belief that a woman can't and should not say 'no' when the man wants sex. Her job is to receive him without resistance
- Only women are expected to be virgins on their wedding night

### 3.2. *Sexual Myths about Women*

- Women do not have sexual temptations
- It is considered to be acceptable for women to use their sexuality to control and punish their husbands
- Pregnant women cannot have sexual relations
- A woman is no longer a virgin if she uses a tampon[7] during her menstrual cycle
- Women are still virgins if they only have anal sex.

## 4. Mode of Infection

HIV is a virus, which infects the cells that make up the human body and replicates within those cells. The immune system is a group of cells and organs that protect the body by fighting against the diseases.

---

6 As a result, there is a lack of respect for women in the sexual realm.

7 A tampon is a mass of cotton or rayon; or a mixture of the two inserted into a body cavity or wound to absorb bodily fluid. Tampons are used as menstrual device which worn completely inside the vaginal canal with the exception of the string, thus they offer discretion and freedom to involve in activities such as swimming and horseback riding without interruption.
http://www.wen.org.uk/gen_eng/Genetics/tampon1.htm (2.10.2010 7pm)

HIV particularly attacks a special type of immune system cell known as CD4 cells (T4cells),[8] a type of white blood cell that makes up a major part of the immune system. Over a period of time, if the CD4 cells are damaged, the body is less capable of protecting the person from bacteria, viruses and fungi, which can lead to infection or illness. It is hard to identify an infected person from his/her external appearance. The patients may look and feel perfectly well for many years and may not know that s/he is infected. However, as the person's immune system weakens, they become increasingly vulnerable to illness.[9]

## 5. Conversion of HIV into AIDS

AIDS is an extremely serious condition, and at this stage, the body has very little defense against any sort of infection. Without drug treatment, HIV infection usually progresses to AIDS in an average of ten years. This average is based on a person having a reasonable diet. Antiretroviral medication[10] can prolong the time between HIV infection and the inception of AIDS. Modern combination therapy is highly effective and theoretically, someone with HIV can live for a long time before it becomes AIDS. These medicines, however, are not widely available in many developing countries around the world.

---

8 CD4 Cell Count – It is a measure of the number of disease-fighting cells in blood. A healthy HIV-uninfected person would normally have at least 500 CD4 cells per microlitre (uL) of blood. The CD4 count gradually falls during HIV infection. Current guidelines generally recommend starting antiretroviral treatment when the CD4 count has fallen below 350 cells/uL. In some situations, antiretroviral medication may be started when CD4 cell counts are higher than 350 cells/uL http://www.tibotec-hiv.com/gldisplay.jhtml?itemname=glossary#gl_Antiretroviralmedications (28.9.2010 5pm)

9 Philip Kuruvilla, *HIV/AIDS: A Hand Book for the Church in India* (Delhi: ISPCK, 2004), 5.

10 Antiretroviral medications are used to retard the development of HIV infection and it also suppresses the effects of virus. In course of time, the patient's immune system can be slowly restored such that he/she can continue to lead a normal and illness-free life.
http://www.suite101.com/content/treatment-for-hivaids-a54642 (29.9.2010 12pm)

As a result, millions of people who cannot access to medication are continuing to die. This medication slows the progression from HIV to AIDS, and keeps some people healthy for many years. In some cases, it seems to stop working after a number of years. On the other hand, people can recover from AIDS and live with HIV for a very long time.[11]

## 6. Symptoms of HIV and AIDS

The primary symptom is that failure of immune system in the body. Because of which bacteria, viruses, fungi and parasites infects the individual's physical condition. HIV damages the immune system and making it not to function properly. Following are the four phases which a HIV positive individual undergoes:

**6.1.** ***Window Period*** – It is the period from infection with HIV till the antibodies are detected using blood test. The virus is hiding in the body, therefore doctors cannot detect it. The HIV test during this phase would be negative. This phase can last 0-6 months. It is possible for a person to infect others at this stage.

**6.2.** ***Asymptomatic Phase*** – The person is free from any sign and symptoms. The virus is present in the body, but the person does not experience any symptoms. Although the person feels healthy, s/he can still infect others. This phase can last for years, despite the fact that sometimes it progresses much quicker.

**6.3.** ***Symptomatic Phase*** – In this period, virus is there in the body, and the person could experience symptoms. The HIV – related symptoms are loss of appetite, swollen glands,[12] fever, night sweats, weight loss, skin rashes, diarrhea, weakness and coughing. Symptoms

---

11 Savitri Ramaiah, *HIV and AIDS,* 11.

12 Gland swelling commonly refers to enlargement of the lymph glands, also known as lymph nodes. Lymph nodes are small rounded or bean-shaped masses of lymphatic tissue surrounded by a capsule of connective tissue. Lymph glands (nodes) are located in many places in the lymphatic system throughout the body.
http://www.medicinenet.com/swollen_lymph_nodes/symptoms.htm (4.10.2010 2.30pm)

and signs can appear from the second month of infection to 10 years or more than that time period. Not all people experience the same signs and symptoms.

**6.4.** ***Full Blown AIDS*** – The person is in the terminal stage of HIV and AIDS, suffering from life-threatening illness. This stage usually lasts one to two years depending on the availability of the treatment. HIV can be transmitted during all four phases, regardless of how the person feels or looks. Someone who has reached this stage of AIDS, with treatment can return to the asymptomatic phase for periods of time.[13]

## 7. Consequences of HIV and AIDS

### 7.1. *The Impact of HIV and AIDS on Agricultural Production*

HIV and AIDS may have disadvantageous impact on rural households' productive capacity. Since the person is infected with HIV, quantity, quality and productivity of house hold labour are highly affected initially. Since women contribute 70 – 80 percent of their time for the agricultural labour force, remaining time could be used for caring sick people and rituals activities.

HIV and AIDS will affect the availability of disposable cash income which could be used for agricultural production. During episodes of illness, household financial resources may be diverted to pay for medical treatment and eventually to meet funeral costs. Such resources may otherwise be used to purchase agricultural inputs, such as occasional extra labour or other complementary inputs (e.g. new seeds or plants, fertilizer, pesticides, etc.). Family assets (e.g. livestock) might be sold off. Some of the effects of labour shortage in full impact communities are:

- Reduction in the acreage of land under cultivation
- Delay in farming operations such as tillage, planting and weeding
- Reduction in the ability to control crop pests
- Decline in crop yields

13 Facilitator's guide, *Prescriptions for Hope* (USA: Samaritan's Purse, 2005), 21-22.

- Loss of soil fertility
- Shift from labour-intensive crops (e.g. banana) to less labour-intensive crops (e.g. sweet potatoes)
- Decline in livestock production; Loss of agricultural knowledge and management skills.[14]

## 7.2. *The Economic Impact*

HIV and AIDS cause a reduced labour supply through increased mortality and illness. Productivity is prone to decline among those who are able to work because of illness related to HIV. Government also faces economic crisis, because government is forced to spend more for the healing of expanding epidemic.[15]

## 7.3. *The Impact on Children*

As parents and family members fall ill, children take up the responsibility to earn which would fetch the need for food, care for family members. These children have less opportunity to adequate nutrition, basic health care, housing and clothing. If both parents are HIV positive, chances are there for the children to become orphan. In some poor households, children[16] are removed from school because of the lack of money to pay for uniform and fees.

## 7.4. *Social Effect of HIV and AIDS*

When the epidemic strikes, people in the surrounding region will also be experiencing social ramifications. If many people are living with HIV in a place, then the moral behavior of all the people in that region will be questioned or even doubted. Community cohesion and the contributions of the community to the larger society have negative impacts.[17] Social factors like stigma and discrimination acts as a major obstacle to pay attention to the sufferers. Moreover, the

14 http://www.fao.org/docrep/x0259e/x0259e02.htm#TopOfPage (4.10.2010 4.30pm)

15 http://www.dosomething.org/actnow/tipsandtools/the-effect-hivaids-society (4.10.2010 6pm)

16 Particularly girl children.

17 http://www.ehow.com/facts_5144656_social-effect-hiv-aids.html (25.10.2010 3pm)

disease is often identified with groups like intravenous drug users (IDUs) and homosexuals who are facing double stigma as a result of HIV.[18]

## 8. Factors that contribute to HIV and AIDS-related stigma

Since HIV and AIDS is a life-threatening disease, many react to it in strong ways. HIV infection is associated with behaviors (such as homosexuality, drug addiction, prostitution or promiscuity) that are already stigmatized. Most people become infected with HIV through sex which often carries moral baggage. Quite often, HIV infection is thought to be the result of personal irresponsibility. Religious or moral beliefs force some people to believe that being infected with HIV is the result of moral fault.

## 9. Forms of Discrimination and Stigmatization

Details of both overt and covert forms Discrimination and Stigmatization are found. Overt forms of discrimination and stigmatization include behaviors that are direct and carried out openly following knowledge of one's stero-status. Few of the overt forms of discrimination experienced by respondents are as below:

### 9.1. *At Home and in the Community*

- Sever relationships, desertion and separation
- Denial of property share and access to finance
- Block access to spouse and children, or other relatives
- Physical separation at home, separate sleeping arrangement
- Obstruct entry to common area, facilities like toilet, etc.
- Stop entry to common places like village or a neighborhood area
- Denial of last rituals
- Passing negative remarks about the positive member (for example: 's/he is paying for the past sin')
- Arousing guilt feeling for jeopardizing the family economy and for degrading family prestige

18 Arvind Singhal & Everett M. Rogers, *Combating AIDS: Communication Strategies in Action* (New Delhi: SAGE Publications, 2003), 242-250.

### 9.2. *In Hospitals*

- Refusal by hospitals/doctors to provide treatment for HIV and AIDS related illness
- Refuse to admit in the hospital for care/treatment
- Refuse to operate or help in operation/surgeries/dressing of wounds
- Blocking access to facilities like common toilet and common vessels
- Physical separation of the person in the ward, separate arrangements for bed outside the ward in a gallery
- Delay in treatment[19]
- Stoppage of ongoing treatment/medication/injections
- Early discharge from the hospital
- Limiting the positive person's movements within the ward/room
- Refusal to lift/touch dead body of positive person
- Covering the body with plastic sheet
- Reluctance in giving services of ambulance facilities

### 9.3. *At the Work Place*

- Removal from employment
- Stoppage of health/insurance facilities
- Maintaining social distance
- Making fun/jeering at
- Covert forms of discrimination and stigmatization also includes those behaviors which are indirect, hidden and more subtle.[20]

## 10. AIDS and LAW

The law has an important role in complementing and assisting education, public health and contributing to generate awareness. It is the role of the legislation to offer non-discrimination and encourage community participation with regard to integration of HIV positive people in the society. This enhances people to place their trust and cooperation on people living with HIV and AIDS

19 Example: made to wait in queues, and asking to come next day/time.

20 Satpathy G. C. *Encyclopedia of AIDS,* Vol. 3 (Delhi: Kalpaz Publications, 2003), 168-170.

without stigmatizing and alienating them.[21] It is the responsibility of the state to enact or strengthen antidiscrimination laws which would protect people living with HIV and AIDS. This will ensure privacy, confidentiality and human concerns to the HIV positive people.[22]

This theme, AIDS and LAW, relates to the need to recognize and distinguish between different levels on which the law can operate in the context of HIV and AIDS policy. The complex social and ethical dimensions of HIV, however, have invited for more creative approaches to define how law can contribute to HIV and AIDS policy. This requires an exploration of not only the proscriptive function of the law but also the ways in which the law can be used - or not used - in a constructive way to promote and reinforce the goals of HIV strategies.[23]

## 10.1. *HIV Legislation*

Even though the drafting of the legislation may be complex, the need cannot be undermined. Complexities may arise, for instance, due to inherent contradictions which demands exceptions. It is because of this reason, drafting of AIDS legislation is done with great care. So that it would meet the needs of the infected and affected. It has to be effective and not self-defeating by driving people who are at risk. The guidelines of WHO, UNAIDS and the Commission of Human Rights are incorporated to the maximum range, inorder to minimize the impact of HIV and AIDS. At the same time, it should not be discriminatory in accordance with United Nations Resolution No. 1995/44 passed by Commission on Human Rights. This resolution calls upon states to ensure laws, policies, and practices in the context of HIV and AIDS and human rights standards including the right to privacy and integrity of people living with HIV and AIDS. It

21 Samiran Panda, Anindya Chatterjee and Abu S. Abdul-Quder, *Living with AIDS Virus: The Epidemic and the Response in India* (New Delhi: SAGE Publications, 2002), 166-167.

22 http://www.ipu.org/PDF/publications/aids_en.pdf (26.10.2010 3pm)

23 P. D. Mathew, "AIDS and LAW" in Women's Link, Vol. 2, No. 4, 1996, 26-28.

prohibits HIV and AIDS related discrimination and guarantees care for the people living with HIV and AIDS.[24]

### 10.2. *The Proscriptive role of the Law*

The impact of the law in its proscriptive mode on HIV and AIDS policy became evident in the epidemic level. The response to the activities that were placing people at risk of HIV infection has been formulated in the context of legal prohibitions. The involvement of the law in HIV and AIDS policy has often hindered rather than effective implementation. The law has presented an obstacle to minimize the spread of HIV and meet the needs of people who are already infected. The coercive nature of the law is to impose criminal sanctions which will reduce the spread of HIV. This may actively hinder prevention by alienating those people who are at risk of HIV. The noteworthy point is that lawmakers must be sensitive to the direct and indirect impact of legal sanctions.[25]

### 10.3. *The Protective role of the Law*

Protective role of the law is to protect individual from harmful and undesirable occurrences. Since discrimination against victims is increasing, laws are employed to protect human rights. Objective of the legislation is to produce respect for individuals and to promote human rights. There are two protective functions of the law which are dominant. They are,

1. Protection against discrimination.
2. Protection of confidentiality for people with HIV.

It must be recognized that both the proscriptive and the protective model for legal intervention involve fundamental value

---

24 Taunya Lovell, "Legal Challenges: State Intervention, Reproduction and HIV-Infected Women," in *HIV/AIDS and Childbearing: Public Policy, Private Lives,* Edited by Ruth R. Faden & Nancy E. Kass (New York: Oxford University Press, 1996), 143-148.

25 Taunya Lovell, "Legal Challenges: State Intervention, Reproduction and HIV-Infected Women," 143-148.

judgments. It also involves the value conflicts in relation to what should be protected and what should be prohibited.[26]

## 10.4. *The Instrumental role of the Law*

When the proscriptive and the protective models of legal intervention focus on the conduct of individuals, instrumental model visualizes a legal response to HIV and AIDS which will operate on a broader and more far-reaching level. This is the model which suggests that the law can play a proactive role, not merely in mediating rights and obligations in the lives of individuals, but also in seeking to change underlying values and patterns of social interaction that create vulnerability to the threat of HIV infection.

## 10.5. *The Potential role of the Law*

The potential role of the law revisits the emerging socio-economic patterns of HIV infection. The rate of new infections is estimated to be almost three times higher among women than among men. It suggests that one of the most significant risk factors for HIV infection relates not to sexual or drug-use activities as such but rather to socio-economic dependency. HIV infection is preventable, for those people who have access to information and means to implement appropriate preventive measures. At this juncture, it is worth to note that people who remain most vulnerable are those who are economically powerless. Due to financial constraints, preventive measures such as condoms are not affordable. The risk of transmission increases because of the non-accessibility to proper health care. Adequate treatment could not be offered to sexually transmitted diseases due to economic crisis. The significant challenge for HIV and AIDS policy is to identify the underlying social and economic factors that deprive individuals to protect themselves against HIV infection. This challenge involves enormous task which could be the scope of HIV and AIDS policy. Nonetheless, efforts to address the socio-economic risk factors for HIV infection are a critical part of an effective strategy to reduce the spread of HIV. Legal systems are established in the developing countries to ensure the reduction

---

26 Satpathy G. C. *Encyclopedia of AIDS*, Vol. 3, 287.

of economic dependence of women through land ownership and marital property laws. This in turn permits women to have access to proper health care and it guarantees economic support. Ultimately, this legal system could equalize the social imbalance which is caused through HIV.[27]

## 11. Women and AIDS

"HIV and AIDS epidemic unfortunately remains as an epidemic of women," says Michel Sidibé, Executive Director of UNAIDS.[28] It was estimated that around 50 percent are women out of 31.3 million adults living with HIV and AIDS in the worldwide. It is suggested that 98 percent of these women are living in developing countries. The AIDS epidemic has a unique impact on women, which has been exacerbated by their role within society and also by their biological vulnerability to HIV infection.

Generally women are at a greater risk of heterosexual transmission of HIV. Biologically women are having high risk of being infected with HIV through unprotected heterosexual intercourse than men. Women have less voice to negotiate about the usage of condom and because more likely they are subjected to non-consensual sex.[29] Women's childbearing role includes the issue of mother-to-child transmission of HIV. The responsibility of caring for AIDS patients and orphans is also an issue that has a greater effect on women.

There are a number of things that can be done in order to reduce the burden of the epidemic among women. These includes,

- promoting and protecting women's human rights
- increasing education and awareness among women

---

27 http://www.undp.org/hiv/publications/issues/english/issue11e.htm#The%20protective%20role%20of%20law (26/10/2010 10:45pm)

28 http://www.un.org/apps/news/story.asp?NewsID=34977&Cr=aids&Cr1 (27/10/2010 12:30pm)

29 Non consensual sex could be equated with rape or sexual assault. Even within the bond of marriage, many women are raped by their own husbands.

- encouraging the development of new preventative technologies such as post-exposure prophylaxis[30] and microbicides[31]
- liberating women within their homes and protecting them outside their home.[32]

## 11.1. *Women, HIV and AIDS - the global picture*

Globally, HIV and AIDS is the leading cause of death among women during reproductive age. The percentage of women living with HIV and AIDS varies significantly between different regions of the world. The percentage is higher in Africa and Asia.

UNAIDS estimates that around 4.7 million adults are living with HIV in Asia, among which approximately 35% are women. Most of the women have only one lifetime sexual partner. But many women are put to risk due to unprotected sex of their husbands outside the marriage or injecting drugs. It has been estimated that 90% of women living with HIV in Asia were infected through their husband. According to the National AIDS Control Organisation (NACO), number of adults living with HIV and AIDS in India is estimated to be 2.4 million and out of which 39.3% are women. As HIV transmission in India is largely through heterosexual contact, the infection rate among women is increasing. Low economic and social status of women continues to be a barrier to prevent new infections.[33]

---

30 Post-exposure prophylaxis (PEP) is short-term antiretroviral treatment to reduce the HIV. http://www.who.int/hiv/topics/prophylaxis/en/ (10/1/2011 8:00pm)

31 Microbicides are compounds that can be applied inside the vagina or rectum to protect against sexually transmitted infections (STIs) including HIV. http://www.who.int/hiv/topics/microbicides/microbicides/en/ (10/1/2011 8:30pm)

32 Rebecca J. Cook, "Human Rights, HIV Infection and Women," in *HIV: Law, Ethics and Human Rights,* Edited by Jayasuriya D. C. (New Delhi: UNDP, 1995), 235–238.

33 Nirmala Skill & Bennet Abraham, "HIV/AIDS: Medical Scenario," in *HIV/ AIDS: A Challenge to Theological Education,* Edited by Samson Prabhakar & George Mathew Nalunnakkal (Bangalore: BTESSC / SATHRI, 2004), 122-123.

## 11.2. *How is the HIV and AIDS epidemic affecting women?*

When a person becomes ill from AIDS, the care is usually a responsibility of woman. She is expected to offer this care in addition to many other household tasks such as cooking, cleaning, and caring the children and the elderly, etc. Caring the ill parents, children or husband is unpaid and can increase the workload of a woman. Oppression of women is highly visible.[34] Women often struggle to fetch an income while providing care. Therefore, many families affected by AIDS suffer from increasing poverty. In some parts of India, family's livelihood relies on growing and maintaining crops, eventually the death of farmers can lead to famine.

The AIDS epidemic also affects young girls and elderly women. Often in households where both parents are ill from AIDS, the responsibility is imposed to the daughter. Sometimes, this responsibility forces her to miss school. If both parents die then it tends to be the grandmothers, aunts or cousins who then look after the orphans. This may lead to increase in child labour in the future.[35]

## 11.3. *Women and Children*

Mother-to-child transmission (MTCT) is an issue that directly affects women and at the same time increases the spread of HIV. MTCT occurs when an HIV positive woman passes the virus to her baby during pregnancy, labour and delivery, or through breastfeeding. UNAIDS say that at the end of 2009 there were an estimated 2.1 million children (under 15 years) living with HIV, most of whom were infected by their mothers. Drugs have been produced to reduce the chances of child being infected with HIV from mother. But these drugs have not reached the grass root level. Drug companies have significantly reduced the price of drugs such as nevirapine[36] and

34 Kenneth R. Overberg, *Ethics & AIDS: Compassion and Justice in Global Crisis* (Mumbai: St. Pauls Press, 2009), 141ff.

35 Overberg R. Kenneth, *Ethics & AIDS: Compassion and Justice in Global Crisis,* 125-126.

36 Nevirapine, also known as Viramune, which is a type of medicine called a non-nucleoside reverse transcriptase inhibitor (NNRTI). NNRTIs block reverse transcriptase, a protein that HIV needs to make more copies of

AZT,[37] which help in preventing HIV transmission from mother to child. However, because of limited human resources and poor infrastructures, many women are still not receiving these drugs.[38]

## 11.4. *Medical differences*

Men and women are liable to suffer from very similar AIDS related illnesses and symptoms. However, there are a few differences between men and women with relation to opportunistic infections and antiretroviral drug treatment. Women could suffer from different opportunistic infections, such as severe pelvic inflammatory disease (PID),[39] recurrent vaginal yeast infections and cancerous changes in the cervix.[40] Side effects of some antiretroviral drugs also differ among men and women. Nevirapine[41] is used for the prevention of HIV transmission from mother-to-child. It can be also used as combination therapy for the treatment of HIV and AIDS. However, Nevirapine sometimes can cause some extreme side effects, such as skin rash and clinical liver toxicity, which in some cases can be life

---

itself. Nevirapine comes in tablet and oral suspension form and is taken by mouth.
http://www.aidsinfo.nih.gov/DrugsNew/DrugDetailNT.aspx?int_id=116 (3/11/2010 8am)

37 AZT stands for AZIDOTHYMIDINE, which is also called as ZIDOVUDINE. This is a drug used to delay the development of AIDS in patients infected with HIV. AZT belongs to the family of nucleoside reverse transcriptase inhibitors (NRTIs).
http://www.britannica.com/EBchecked/topic/46868/AZT (3/11/2010 11am)

38 Ruth R. Faden & Nancy E. Kass, *HIV,AIDS and Childbearing: Public Policy, Private Lives* (New York: Oxford University Press, 1996), 428–430.

39 Pelvic inflammatory disease (PID) is the infection or inflammation of upper genital tract, i.e., the ovary, the fallopian tubes and the uterus.
http://www.whereincity.com/medical/topic/women-health/diseases/pelvic-inflammatory-disease-10.htm (4/11/2010 10.30pm)

40 The cervix is the lower end of the uterus. It is considered to be the neck for uterus.
http://www.nlm.nih.gov/medlineplus/ency/article/002317.htm (4/11/2010 11.15pm)

41 It is an Antiretroviral drug.

threatening. HIV positive women experience changes in menstrual patterns. Amenorrhea is the situation where women experience the loss of heavy blood flow. This is quite commonly reported among HIV positive women. Other menstrual problems include irregular periods, missed periods, abnormal bleeding and more extreme cases of premenstrual syndrome (PMS).[42]

## 12. Why is it difficult for women to protect themselves from HIV infection?

### 12.1. *Inequalities within the Family*

Women enjoy few rights within sexual relationships and within family in some societies. Often men make the majority of decisions, such as whom they will marry and whether they will have more than one sexual partner, etc. This power imbalance makes it more difficult for women to protect themselves from getting infected with HIV. For example, a woman may not be able to insist on the use of a condom if her husband is the one who makes the decisions. Marriage does not always protect a woman from becoming infected with HIV. Many new infections occur within marriage or long-term relationships as a result of unfaithful partners.[43]

### 12.2. *Violence against Women*

Women who are victims of sexual violence are at a higher risk of being exposed to HIV. Women become more vulnerable to infection, because of the lack of condom use and forcible nature of rape. In India, it has been witnessed that HIV transmission is higher among

42 Premenstrual syndrome (PMS) is a combination of emotional, physical, psychological, and mood disturbances that occur after a woman's ovulation and typically ending with the onset of her menstrual flow. http://www.medicinenet.com/premenstrual_syndrome/article.htm (4/11/2010 11.50pm)

43 Somen Das, *Woman in India* (Calcutta: ISPCK, 1997), 40ff.

abusive husbands than non-abusive husbands.[44] So the level of victimization of women continues to grow higher.[45]

In countries where armed conflict is widespread, there have been reports of rape being used as a 'tool of war'. Amnesty International reported that between 1999 and 2000 in every armed conflict that they investigated, the torture of women was reported.[46]

### 12.3. *Women's inheritance and property rights*

Women do not have the same property rights as men in many countries. Especially in India, property is typically owned by men. Even after marriage, women don't enjoy the property rights as like their husbands. When the husband dies, his property goes to the side of his family and not to his wife. This is the pitiable condition of the inheritance rights which continues to be discriminatory. The denial of woman's inheritance and property rights can increase her vulnerability to HIV. Women have limited economic stability, because of impossibility to own property. This can lead to an increased risk of sexual exploitation and violence. This forces women to undergo abusive relationships or resort to informal sex work for economic survival.[47]

## 13. Human Rights and AIDS

### 13.1. *History of Human Rights Law*

During the formative phase of modern international law, European religious authorities have endorsed Natural law principles. These principles allows nation to intervene in the domestic affairs of other nation. If a state dealt inhumanly in its territory with the nationals of another state, however, the national state had legal rights of humanitarian intervention.

---

44 http://journals.lww.com/jaids/Abstract/2009/08150/Intimate_Partner_Violence_Functions_as_Both_a_Risk.13.aspx (6/11/2010 11.15am)

45 Lakshmi Misra, *Women's Issues: An Indian Perspective* (New Delhi: Northern Book Centre, 1992), 1–2.

46 http://www.amnestyusa.org/women/rapeinwartime.html (6/11/2010 11.35am)

47 http://www.avert.org/women-hiv-aids.htm (8/11/2010 01:02 pm)

Through the series of international agreements in the beginning of the present century, women's special needs of international protection were recognized. Their aim was not to liberate women within their homes, but rather to protect them from sexual and other personal vulnerability that might diminish the integrity of family units. The *International Convention Respecting Prohibition of Night Work for Women in Industrial Employment* in 1906 was the first of a series of international conventions. It was supported by the International Labour Office, protecting women in the workforce. This has been reinforced by yet another convention called, *Convention Concerning the Employment of Women Before and After Childbirth* in 1919. Similarly, the *International Convention for the Suppression of Traffic in Women and Children* in 1921 was the first of a series of international conventions reflecting humane and moral concerns for protection of women and families.[48]

### 13.2. *International Foundations of Human Rights Law*

Modern international human rights law has founded the regional and subject-specific conventions which were inspired by the Universal Declaration of Human Rights. The general conventions are,

- *International Covenant on Civil and Political Rights*
- *International Covenant on Economic, Social and Cultural Rights*

Two major leading specialized conventions are,

- *International Convention on the Elimination of All Forms of Discrimination against Women*
- *Convention on the Rights of the Child*

It is essential to observe the functional interdependence of individual rights in view of the socio-economic and cultural dimensions of women's health status. In the Fourth World Conference on Women held at Beijing in 1995, improving the status of women within sexual relationships was underscored. This conference further

48 Rebecca J. Cook, "HIV: Ethics and Human Rights", 136.

explained that "the human rights of women include their right to have control and decide freely and responsibly on matters related to their sexuality, free of bullying, discrimination and violence. Equal relationships between women and men in matters of sexual relations and reproduction, including full respect for the integrity of the person, requiring mutual respect, consent and shared responsibility for sexual behavior and its consequences."[49]

## 13.3. *The Duty of Nondiscrimination*

The most basic human right in social existence is the duty of nondiscrimination. International Conference on Population and Development held at Cairo states regarding women's health that a state of complete physical, mental and social well-being and not merely the absence of disease or infirmity. This further includes all matters relating to the reproductive system and to its function and process. This international legal order opines that women have authority to have safe sex and freedom to decide on reproduction. But in reality, many women are discriminated and they do not have power over their sexuality.[50]

Many disadvantages that affect women's health arise from gender discrimination in their social circumstances and from political, economic, spiritual and other sources of subordination. It affects their self-determination and their self-esteem, creating frustration and depression reflected in a lack of mental and social well-being. Sex is a matter of biological classification, but gender is a social construct applied by human societies. This construction is made through the social institutions like, family, culture, religion, etc. Authority is seen as male gendered. Moreover, this has been credibly exercised by such male gendered institutions like, governments, military

---

49 Bayer R. Levine & Walf S. M., *HIV Antibody Screening: An Ethical Framework for Evaluating Proposed Programs* (Journal of American Medical Association 1986), 64–68.

50 *Institute of Medicine and the National Academy of Sciences: Confronting AIDS* (Washington DC: National Academy Press, 1989), 11ff.

administrations, religious judicial, academicians and professionals such as physicians and lawyers.[51]

Sex and gender discrimination continue to operate in modern times to predispose women with high levels of HIV infection and AIDS. A stereotype of young women is that they are sexually timid and passive, and that only loose girls prepare themselves for sexual activity. When women are uneducated and illiterate, they have few means of sustaining themselves outside their parents' homes. Their employment opportunities are limited, confined to service functions like domestic works, etc. Usually they are paid very less and which results in economic crisis. This ultimately forces them to sell their sexuality in prostitution.[52]

More traditional gender discrimination often compounds women's vulnerability to HIV infection and AIDS. Possibly, they are married at early ages to older men. Soon they face early widowhood. They do not enjoy legal widow's rights of land and property inheritance. They become a burden to husband's families and communities. They are even unable to rejoin to their birth families.[53] To solve these issues, women should not be discriminated on the ground of gender.

## 14. The Protected Human Rights

### 14.1. *The Rights to Life and Survival*

Initially this right was universally declared for political and children convention. But after the tragic record of death due to HIV and AIDS, considerable scope was installed to enlarge and enhance legal claims for AIDS sufferers which would develop care to prolong the

51 WCC Study Document, *Facing AIDS: The Challenge, The Church's Response* (Geneva: WCC Publications, 1997), 73–75.

52 Sujatha Gothoskar, *Struggles of Women at Work* (New Delhi: Vikas Publishing House Pvt Ltd, 1992), 1ff.

53 Samiran Panda, Anindya Chatterjee and Abu S. Abdul-Queder, *Living with AIDS Virus: The Epidemic and the Response in India,* 168–171.

life. This right condemns the premature death and guarantees denial of right to death.[54]

## 14.2. *The Rights to Health Care*

In the Economic Covenant, it is addressed that Article 12 (1) recognizes "the right of everyone to the enjoyment of the highest attainable standard of physical and mental health." This Article reveals that health care includes,

- Two major leading specialized conventions are, avoidance of HIV infection,
- Two major leading specialized conventions are, maintenance of a symptom-free condition,
- Two major leading specialized conventions are, free from mental deterioration and clinical depression, etc.

This right gives choice to women living with HIV and AIDS to decide whether to undertake pregnancy or not. This right further describes that "States Parties shall take all appropriate measures to eliminate discrimination against women in the field of health care in order to ensure access to health care services including those related to family planning."[55]

## 14.3. *The Right to Liberty and Security of the Person*

As per the Universal Declaration, right to liberty and security concentrates on the removal of unlawful exercise of governmental power. In the context of HIV infection, rights to liberty and security may appear personal rather than political. This right closely intersects the right to health care when governmental policies deny individuals the means to protect themselves against infection.[56]

54 Rebecca J. Cook, *Human Rights of Women: National and International Perspectives* (Philadelphia: Pennsylvania Press, 1994), 499–500.

55 Rebecca J. Cook, "HIV: Ethics and Human Rights," 247–248.

56 Rebecca J. Cook, "HIV: Ethics and Human Rights," 250–251.

### 14.4. *The Right to Freedom from Torture or Ill Treatment*

Human Rights considered rape as torture which provokes transmission of HIV to victims. Torture tends to be understood as willful brutality imposed through direct or indirect pursuit of a public or political purpose. Women face multiple vulnerabilities to sexuality. Instead of recognizing their rights, they are exposed to torture. In order to impose ethnic dominance among women, tortures may be instigated. This is condemned by this right.[57] Women's victimization is aggravated not only by the risk of HIV infection, but also being isolated by families and communities. Moreover, involuntary loss of virginity is stigmatized for women and not for men. In many work environments, women become vulnerable to sexual harassment including intercourse they cannot resist because of their economic dependency on their employers. Beyond this, they may be compelled to conceal infection and their health vulnerability and perhaps forego necessary treatment, lest they may forfeit their employment. Enforcement of human rights laws against industrial and related ill-treatment would empower such women to preserve their health interests, employment and integrity.[58]

### 14.5. *The Right to Marry and Find a Family*

Right to marry and be part of a family is the constant reaction of human rights professionals. Some jurisdictions have reacted to HIV infection by mandating that an HIV test be made a condition to marry. The right to found a family is necessary for mothers to survive during pregnancy and childbirth. The capacity for procreation is normally a negative right, in which no one is to interfere with conception, pregnancy or adoption; and the government to provide medical treatment, including reproductive technologies in case of infertility. Pregnant women who are living with HIV have the same right to prenatal care, assistance in labour and postnatal care

---

57 International Human Rights Law Group. No justice, no peace: accountability for rape and gendered-based violence in the former Yugoslavia. *Hasting Women's Law Journal,* 2004, 5. http://www.hastingswomenslj.org/ (15/11/2010 11am)

58 Rebecca J. Cook, "HIV: Ethics and Human Rights," 254–255.

as uninfected women, and their children are entitled to the same standard of care as those of uninfected mothers.[59]

## 15. Religion and AIDS

In Christian understanding, the concept of sin is highlighted when an individual is infected with HIV and AIDS. But this notion cannot be applicable to all those who live with HIV and AIDS. There are many women who received this illness from their husbands. Having sexual relations with the marital partner is nothing wrong. But it is due to the illegal sexual relationship of the husbands outside the marriage life becomes the cause for this sickness.[60]

### 15.1. *Dual Role of Religion*

Due to the development of consciousness about the impact of HIV and AIDS, religious teachings have become more conducive to address the issue of HIV and AIDS. But sometime, religion acts like two sides of the same coin. One side it says about loving, embracing, caring, listening,[61] etc., but on the other side, it stigmatizes, discriminates and makes judgments on the basis of morality.[62] There are two approaches employed by the church. One is *rejecting punitive approach*[63] and other is *approach of qualified acceptance.*[64] This dual approach stands as a challenge at large to the theologians and church leaders.[65]

---

59 Rebecca J. Cook, "HIV: Ethics and Human Rights," 258.

60 Sahu Sathyarthi & Sahu Sarah, *Counsel for Crisis Times* (Delhi: Cambridge Press, 2009), 75.

61 Daniela Gennrich, *The Church in an HIV+ World: A Practical Handbook* (South Africa: Cluster Publications, 2004), 40.

62 Kurin Manoj, "Biblical Perspective on the Churches Response to HIV/AIDS and Its Visible Manifestation" in *HIV/AIDS: A Hand Book for the Church in India*, Edited by Philip Kuruvilla (Delhi: ISPCK, 2004), 70.

63 This approach rejects people living with HIV and AIDS basing on the ground of illness by stating it as a result of sin.

64 This approach accepts HIV and AIDS as part of reality and stretch the hand of compassion to support them to cope with the disease.

65 Monica Jyotsna Melanchthon, "Facing HIV and AIDS: Some Insights from the Hebrew Bible" in *HIV/AIDS: A Challenge to Theological Education,* Edited

## 15.2. *HIV and Sin*

It is a misleading judgmental view of saying that HIV and AIDS is a result of Sin. Basically sin is an individual's failure to live up to the standards of conduct, violation of laws or moral codes. Christianity sees sin as a deliberate violation of the will of God and as being attributable to human pride, self-centeredness and disobedience.[66]

## 15.3. *Usage of Scripture to address HIV and AIDS*

Faith communities read the scripture for guidance, comfort, inspiration and to obtain wisdom. Christians scrutinize Bible to seek advices and answers to the difficulties which occurs in life. Some of the stories in the OT like Miriam's skin ailment, Naaman's skin ailments are re-read to cull out new meanings which would instill hope among people living with HIV and AIDS.[67] The Hebrew Bible also uses the following terms to prescribe ill health. חָלָה[68] *chalah* "to be weak, sick"; חֳלִי[69] *choli* "weakness, illness"; דָּוָה[70] *dawah* "to be ill, unwell"; דְּוַי[71] *dewaj* "faintness, sickness". Some of the words which are used for healing are, חָיָה[72] *chajah* "to live, to revive"; שׁוּב[73] *shub* "to return, to restore"; רָפָא[74] *rafa'* "to heal,"[75] etc. This ensures that scripture can be used to address the issue of HIV and AIDS in the

---

by Samson Prabhakar & George Mathew Nalunnakkal (Bangalore: BTESSC / SATHRI, 2004), 77.

66 Kurin Manoj, "Biblical Perspective on the Churches Response to HIV/AIDS and Its Visible Manifestation," 71.

67 Musimbi R. A. Kanyoro, "Reading the Bible in the face of HIV/AIDS" in *Grant me Justice! HIV/AIDS & Gender Readings of the Bible*, Edited by Musa W. Dube and Musimbi R. A. Kanyoro (South Africa: Cluster Publications, 2004), viii.

68 BDB, 318.

69 BDB, 318.

70 BDB, 188.

71 BDB, 188.

72 BDB, 311.

73 BDB, 1000.

74 BDB, 951.

75 Johana Stienert, "Does the Hebrew Bible have anything to tell us about HIV/AIDS?" in *HIV/AIDS and the Curriculum: Methods of Integrating HIV/*

contemporary world. Bible also tells the story of God's ongoing concern for creation and humanity. God's abiding concern related to humanity is well-being or fullness of life. God's love and justice to redeem creation and humanity is also visible in the Bible. So these insights gained from contextual theologies needs to be employed to deepen the understandings and to work for people living with HIV and AIDS.

## 15.4. *Interpreting the Bible*

Traditionally, Bible has been often read and interpreted in such a way to stigmatize, exclude people living with HIV and AIDS. Biblical faith understands sin as breaking the relationship with God and creation. Therefore causing alienation, estrangement, rejection, and stigmatization to God's creation, becomes outcome of sin. Like the same by using the tools of interpretations, concept of sin and stigmatization needs to be redefined for embracing the suffering community.[76]

## Conclusion

This chapter elaborately gives the picture about HIV and AIDS and how it is transmitted among individuals. It suggests how women are treated when they are found HIV+. The consequences which are faced by women are also illustrated. Brief dealing about the religious voices and outlook towards the women living with HIV and AIDS has been discussed. It also depicts how the laws operate and different rights are ensured for women. Another great development is the inception of human rights which is guaranteed for women living with HIV and AIDS.

---

*AIDS in Theological Programmes,* Edited by Musa W Dube (Geneva: WCC Publications, 2003), 25–26.

76 Samson Prabhakar & George Mathew Nalunnakkal, *ed, HIV/AIDS: A Challenge to Theological Education* (Bangalore: BTESSC / SATHRI, 2004), 136-142.

# Chapter 2

# Exegetical Study of Select Passages

## Introduction

Biblical text has been utilized to bring a change in the human attitudes. This chapter attempts to re-read select passages in the context of HIV and AIDS. Aim of integrating HIV and AIDS into biblical studies is to contribute towards prevention, provision of quality care, elimination of the stigma and discrimination. Bible is read not only as a historical and ancient book, but with an eye to current concerns. Exegetical and theological study is carried out along with reader response method on three passages from the Hebrew Bible, i.e., Numbers 12.10-16, 2 Kings 5.8-14 and Ezekiel 37.1-14.[77] The first two passages deal with skin ailments and seem to raise issues related to stigma and discrimination. The last passage pertains to death and life which is significant in the high incidence of death (both physical and metaphorical) that surrounds the epidemic. This would help in contributing new insights to address HIV and AIDS in the present day.

---

77 Selection of three passages is based on the preferential interest of the researcher.

# Numbers 12:10-16

## 1. Translation

### V. 10

וְהֶעָנָ֗ן סָ֚ר מֵעַ֣ל הָאֹ֔הֶל וְהִנֵּ֥ה מִרְיָ֖ם מְצֹרַ֣עַת כַּשָּׁ֑לֶג וַיִּ֧פֶן אַהֲרֹ֛ן אֶל־מִרְיָ֖ם
וְהִנֵּ֥ה מְצֹרָֽעַת׃

When the cloud turned away from upon the tent, and behold, Miriam became leprous like the snow and Aaron turned towards Miriam and behold she was leprous.

### V. 11

וַיֹּ֥אמֶר אַהֲרֹ֖ן אֶל־מֹשֶׁ֑ה בִּ֣י אֲדֹנִ֔י אַל־נָ֨א תָשֵׁ֤ת עָלֵ֙ינוּ֙ חַטָּ֔את אֲשֶׁ֥ר נֹאַ֖לְנוּ
וַאֲשֶׁ֥ר חָטָֽאנוּ׃

And Aaron said to Moses, O my Adonai, I pray now, do not punish us for the sin which we have acted foolishly and sinned.

### V. 12

אַל־נָ֥א תְהִ֖י כַּמֵּ֑ת אֲשֶׁ֤ר בְּצֵאתוֹ֙ מֵרֶ֣חֶם אִמּ֔וֹ וַיֵּאָכֵ֖ל חֲצִ֥י בְשָׂרֽוֹ׃

Let her not be as dead,[78] of whom the flesh is half eaten when he comes out of his mother's womb.

### V. 13

וַיִּצְעַ֣ק מֹשֶׁ֔ה אֶל־יְהוָ֖ה לֵאמֹ֑ר אֵ֕ל נָ֖א רְפָ֥א נָ֖א לָֽהּ׃

And Moses cried to Yahweh saying, "God, heal her I plead"

### V. 14

וַיֹּ֨אמֶר יְהוָ֜ה אֶל־מֹשֶׁ֗ה וְאָבִ֙יהָ֙ יָרֹ֤ק יָרַק֙ בְּפָנֶ֔יהָ הֲלֹ֥א תִכָּלֵ֖ם שִׁבְעַ֣ת יָמִ֑ים
תִּסָּגֵ֞ר שִׁבְעַ֤ת יָמִים֙ מִח֣וּץ לַֽמַּחֲנֶ֔ה וְאַחַ֖ר תֵּאָסֵֽף׃

And Yahweh said to Moses, but if her father spit on her face, would she not be humiliated for seven days? Let her be shut up outside the camp for seven days and after that she may assemble.

---

78 LXX adds ὡσεὶ ἔκτρωμα which means "like ultimate birth". This has been probably used as an emphatic gloss.

## V. 15

וַתִּסָּגֵר מִרְיָם מִחוּץ לַמַּחֲנֶה שִׁבְעַת יָמִים וְהָעָם לֹא נָסַע עַד־הֵאָסֵף מִרְיָם׃

So Miriam was shut out of the camp for seven days and the people did not set out to assemble until Miriam was brought in again.[79]

## V. 16

וְאַחַר נָסְעוּ הָעָם מֵחֲצֵרוֹת וַיַּחֲנוּ בְּמִדְבַּר פָּארָן׃

After that the people set out from Hazeroth, and encamped in the wilderness of Paran.

## 2. Source

Numbers 12.10-16 belongs to an early narrative of J/E. Basing on the occurrence of the word הָעָם "the people", it is decisive that it could be partly from P source.[80] Gray opines that verses 10-15 belong to J/E source. While Gray has not differentiated between J and E, Wenham has attempts to distinguish between the two and suggests that the narrative belongs to the E source.[81] Oesterley and Theodore are of the opinion that v. 1 – 15 fit into E source and 16a & 16b into J & P respectively.[82]

79 LXX has 'was cleansed'. This connects with the isolation which is prescribed in the book of Leviticus about the ritual of cleaning the leper.

80 Philip J. Budd, *Numbers* WBC, Vol. 5 (Dallas, Texas: Word Books Publisher, 1998), 133.

81 Gordon J. Wenham, *Numbers* (England: Sheffield Academic Press, 1997), 71-73.

82 Oesterley E. & Theodore H., *An Introduction to the Books of the Old Testament* (London: Macmillan Company, 1949), 38.

## 3. Structure

| | |
|---|---|
| People complain | 12:1 - 2a |
| Lord hears | 12:2b – 8 |
| Lord is angry and punishes | 12:9 – 10 |
| Appeal to Moses | 12:11-12 |
| Moses' intercession | 12:13 |
| Judgment ceases | 12:14-15[83] |
| Description | 12:6 |

## 4. Literary Context

The people were dissatisfied and unhappy with the leadership which is made known to the reader before and after chapter 12. Chapter 11 portrays the people's popular rebellion arising out of frustration and dissatisfaction with having to eat manna daily. Moses had trouble in handling the people, so he appoints seventy leaders to share the burden. In chapter 13, Moses sends twelve spies in order to study the Land of Canaan. Midrash connects the three texts on Miriam, Eldad and Spies under the category that they spoke against God.[84]

## 5. Explanation

Chapter 12 wraps up the discussion on Moses' leadership. The subject matter of rebellion against proper authority comes to the surface again. In chapter 11, people were complaining in the desert and rebelled against Moses. Except Moses, no other leaders were involved in this struggle. But in the 12th chapter, Moses' family members rebelled against him.[85] In explaining about the family of Moses, Miriam was referred to as the sister of Aaron and Moses in Numbers 26.59.[86] She was never referred directly as a sister of Moses,

83 Gordon J. Wenham, *Numbers*, 51.

84 Graetz Naomi, "Did Miriam Talk Too Much?" *The Feminist Companion to the Bible*, edited by Athalya Brenner (England: Sheffield Academic Press, 1994), 236.

85 Ashley R. Timothy, *The Book of Numbers* (Michigan: Eerdmans, 1993), 222.

86 Henriette Howarth, *The Breaking of Her Dawn: Six Bible Studies from the Old Testament* (Hyderabad: YWCA, 2000), 121.

but as the sister of Aaron. Since Aaron was the brother of Moses, one can assume that she was the sister of Moses.[87]

The meaning of the name 'Miriam' is uncertain. Probably it could mean "beloved."[88] Other meanings which have evolved from the name Miriam are "bitterness" and "rebellion."[89] The Song of Miriam at the Crossing of the Sea is one of the oldest texts in the Old Testament.[90] She has been a great encourager in leading the community to celebrate victory. It is the role of the Prophet to make the people to turn towards God. Miriam took a tambourine in her hand, and all the women went out after her music and danced for the song sung by Miriam for God's glory.[91] Basing on her ministry among many women, she has been acknowledged as a prophet,[92] and she was not called to be a judge over the nation.[93] According to Midrash, Since Pharaoh was killing children, Moses' father was planning not to have any more children. But Miriam is said to have remained him about God's expectation – "be fruit and multiply". This God who expects would protect from any harm that attacks the child. She is a prophet and father listened to her. She therefore she stood far off[94] and watched to see if her prophecy would come true or not.[95]

Hebrew word "Prophetess" means a woman who is inspired to teach the will of God. It is also used for wife of a prophet, and is

---

87 cf. Exodus 2:4; 6:16; 15:20.

88 This meaning has resemblance to the meaning of the name Moses.

89 Herbert Lockyer, *The Women of the Bible* (Michigan: Zondervan Publishing House, 1967), 111.

90 Exodus 15:20 - 21.

91 Phyllis Trible, *Texts of Terror* (Philadelphia: Fortress Press, 1984), 100.

92 The prophet has a ministry of imagination, leading the people to understand their present experience. Elizabeth Cady Stanton, *The Woman's Bible* (Seattle: Task force on Women and Religion, 1974), 101.

93 James B. Hurley, *Man and Woman in Biblical Perspective: A Study in Role Relationships and Authority* (England: InterVarsity Press, 1981), 47–48.

94 cf. Exodus 2:4.

95 Cheryl Exum, "You Shall Let Every Daughter Live: A Study of Exodus 1:8 – 2:10" in *Feminist Companion to Exodus to Deuteronomy*, edited by Athalya Brenner (England: Sheffield Academic Press, 1994), 54.

sometimes applied to a singer of hymns. Here, the first meaning could be applied to Miriam because there is no Biblical record which says that Miriam was ever married.[96] There were five persons[97] identified as prophets prior to Monarchy. Miriam and Deborah were playing prominent roles by taking leadership in the religion of Yahweh.[98] The function of a prophet is to be a messenger for God[99] and to be involves in saving acts. Miriam, along with her mother Jochebed,[100] helped in saving the life of Moses by hiding him in a basket among the reeds (Exodus 2:1 – 10).[101] She is in equal rank with Moses and Aaron in birth and death.[102] She was being chosen and qualified by the Lord to assist in the redemption of God's people.[103] The prophet Micah recognized the significant role of Miriam, by saying that she was called by God to lead Israel out of Egypt along with her brothers Aaron and Moses (Micah 6:4).[104] Noth assumes that Miriam has the characteristic of ecstasy, because ecstasy and cultic songs have a close relationship.[105]

---

96 Edith opines basing on some tradition that, Miriam became wife of Hur, who with Aaron held up the hands of Moses. The Midrash has that she was married to Caleb. But no records are found to confirm either if these traditions. Edith Deen, *All of the Women of the Bible* (San Francisco: Harper & Row Publication, 1983), 58.

97 Abraham, Aaron, Moses, Miriam and Deborah.

98 Deborah M. Gill and Barbara Cavaness, *God's Women: Then and Now* (Secunderabad: Authentic Media, 2007), 217.

99 Irene Nowell OSB, *Women in the Old Testament* (Minnesota: Liturgical Press, 1997), 51-52.

100 Moses' mother is named Jochebed in Exodus 6:16-20 and Numbers 26:58-59. These passages come from the later Priestly tradition that commonly gave names to previously unnamed figures who were significant for Israel's story. Irene Nowell OSB, *Women in the Old Testament*, 49.

101 Deborah M. Gill and Barbara Cavaness, *God's Women: Then and Now*, 49.

102 Alice L. Laffey, *An Introduction to the Old Testament: A Feminist Perspective* (Philadelphia: Fortress Press, 1988), 55.

103 Abraham Kuyper, *Women of the Old Testament* (Michigan: Zondervan Publishing House, 1976), 60.

104 Deborah M. Gill and Barbara Cavaness, *God's Women: Then and Now*, 49.

105 Martin Noth, *Exodus* (London: SCM Press, 1962), 123.

In Numbers 12, Miriam confronts the religious leadership of Moses. In general, God speaks through Miriam, Aaron and other prophets, but Moses was considered to be the primary witness. God speaks to Moses face to face. Any confrontation against Moses' leadership is offensively penalized.[106] Miriam was not exempted from this penalization. She was struck with leprosy. Moses and Aaron remembered the goodness of their sister toward them and interceded to God on behalf of Miriam.[107] All skin diseases are usually temporary. It demands the sufferer to be confined outside the camp.[108] Miriam is separated from the community, but the community did not start their journey until the restoration of Miriam's health.[109] Miriam was placed outside the community for seven days. Number seven is considered to be the symbolic number of completion and it refers to the duration of an appropriate time.[110] During these seven days, she was retreating herself and turned to God for reconciliation.[111] For Miriam, to be healed of leprosy must have been like being born anew.[112] She was healed, but she lost her position of leadership.[113] There was also no further evidence for the prophetic activities of Miriam.[114]

---

106 Numbers 16:1-17:15.

107 Margaret Wold, *Women of Faith & Spirit: Profiles of Fifteen Biblical Witnesses* (Minneapolis: Augsburg Publishing House, 1987), 41.

108 Leviticus 13:4-6.

109 Irene Nowell OSB, *Women in the Old Testament*, 53.

110 Alice L. Laffey, *An Introduction to the Old Testament: A Feminist Perspective,* 54.

111 Theodor Algot Lundholm, *Women of the Bible.* (Illinois: Augustana Book Concern, 1948), 54–55.

112 Daniel Premkumar, *Ronnie's Bible* (Kilpauk: AIDS DESK, 2007), 17.

113 Margaret Wold, *Women of Faith & Spirit: Profiles of Fifteen Biblical Witnesses,* 41.

114 Athalya Brenner, *The Israelite Woman: Social Role and Literary Type in Biblical Narrative* (England: JSOT Press, 1985), 61.

## 6. Was Miriam a born leader or a chosen leader? or both?

Miriam was the first poetess[115] and single woman leader[116] in the Old Testament. Miriam is known as a Prophet (Exodus 15:20) and a leader of Israel (Micah 6:4).[117] Her interest was national and her mission was patriotic.[118] According to the Midrash, she was a role model. She was an advocate of the Biblical command to 'be fruitful and multiply'. That's why she was criticizing Moses for not having sexual relations with his wife. She was encouraging the Israelite males to marry when they were in Egypt and to have many offspring.[119] She apparently knew that she was different from the women around her. In a day when marriage was the vocational destiny for women in Israel, she never married.[120] She would have believed that her destiny lay with the family of Israel rather than with a husband and children of her own. Initially she has absorbed her leadership role for the liberation of her people. In Exodus 15, she was singing and dancing leading the Israelite women in singing praises to God[121] in public.[122] But since she is also the product of a patriarchal society, she is not

115 Herbert Lockyer, *The Women of the Bible,* 112.

116 Deborah M. Gill and Barbara Cavaness, *God's Women: Then and Now,* 52.

117 Henriette Howarth, *The Breaking of Her Dawn: Six Bible Studies from the Old Testament,* 121.

118 Edith Deen, *All of the Women of the Bible* (San Francisco: Harper & Row Publication, 1983), 57.

119 Naomi Graetz, "Did Miriam Talk Too Much," 233.

120 Midrash also claims that Miriam was one of the virtuous midwives. Shiprah and Puah were none other than Jochebed and the 5 year old Miriam. She reprimanded her father when he sought to divorce his wife in response to the Pharaoh's decree to kill the baby boys who were born to Israelites. For Rabbis, Miriam was a perfect role model. The only problem was that she was never known to have married and hence the rabbis marry her off to Caleb. Exodus 1:21 - "he built them houses" is understood to be that they became founders of royal families. Miriam and Caleb together are presented as ancestors of King David. Therefore, Amran's linage is continued.
Naomi Graetz, "Did Miriam Talk Too Much," 234.

121 Margaret Wold, *Women of Faith & Spirit: Profiles of Fifteen Biblical Witnesses,* 40.

122 Kaiser C. Walter, *Toward Old Testament Ethics* (Michigan: Zondervan Publishing House, 1983), 207.

given full credit for the song of victory.[123] Her words and actions were full of motivation to God and because of which she has been brought as a leader and pattern to the women of Israel.[124] In the context of Numbers 12, it is Yahweh who inflicted illness upon her and it is Yahweh who restored her health and made the people to wait till the day of restoration.[125] Other than the incident in Numbers 12,[126] she would be one of the few women in the Bible about whom Rabbis have nothing bad to say.[127] Historians remember the leadership of Miriam and include her as the only woman in the list of descendants of Levi. (1 Chronicles 6.3)[128]

## 7. Comments

### Verse 10

When Yahweh departs and the cloud lifts, Miriam is obsessed with צָרַעַת. The ailment leaves her as white as snow כַּשָּׁלֶג.[129] The same description is used in Exodus 4:6 where Moses' hand was affected with skin ailment at Sinai and 2 Kings 5:27 where Gehazi, Elisha's servant was also penalized with skin ailment.[130] Snaith argues that the skin ailment of Miriam was not exactly true leprosy. This argument is based on the Levitical descriptions of 'leprous uncleanness'. If a person is white all over his body, he/she is ritually clean. But the Hebrew text does not say 'white as snow', merely 'as snow'. Snow is moist and wet. Therefore, it could mean an open wound or ulcer. But as per v.12, Miriam's flesh has been half consumed, which could

---

123 Alice L. Laffey, *An Introduction to the Old Testament: A Feminist Perspective,* 55.

124 Herbert Lockyer, *The Women of the Bible,* 112.

125 Monica Jyotsna Melanchthon, "Facing HIV and AIDS: Some Insights from the Hebrew Bible," in *HIV / AIDS: A Challenge to Theological Education,* edited by Samson Prabhakar & George Mathew Nalunnakkal (Bangalore: BTESSC / SATHRI, 2004), 82.

126 It is the context where Miriam asserts herself and attacks Moses.

127 Naomi Graetz, "Did Miriam Talk Too Much," 235.

128 Margaret Wold, *Women of Faith & Spirit: Profiles of Fifteen Biblical Witnesses,* 41.

129 To the ordinary readers, White as snow is a description which adds horror to the ailment. It is suggested that it could be a form of leprosy.

130 Ashley R. Timothy, *The Book of Numbers,* 227.

be an effect of true leprosy.[131] According to Talmud, there were seven sins which incurred leprosy. They are denunciation, bloodshed, false oaths, immorality, haughtiness, robbery and grudging.[132] In Miriam's case, the only act that she committed was challenging the religious leadership of Moses.[133] But here the word leprous covers a wide range of skin diseases.[134]

## Verses 11-13

בִּי אֲדֹנִי 'O my Adonai' is an expression of profound respect which is used to address God.[135] In this context, Aaron intercedes along with Moses who in turn intercedes with Yahweh for Miriam's restoration.[136] Moses takes an active role only here in this whole narrative.[137] Disasters are being averted through the intercession of Moses.[138] God immediately offered healing to Miriam by answering for the supplication made by Moses. But the Lord insists that she must live outside the camp for seven days.[139]

## Verse 14

Miriam was being humiliated by mere isolation from the community. This forces her to be outside the camp for seven days.[140] יָרֹק יָרַק בְּפָנֶיהָ "spit on her face" - The reappearance of יָרַק is emphatic. It refers to the degrading custom which would cause Miriam to hide or be excluded.[141] Father spitting on the face of a girl was already present.

---

131 N. H. Snaith, *Leviticus and Numbers* (London: Thomas Nelson Printers, 1967), 236.

132 Elliott Binns, *The Book of Numbers* (London: Methuen & Co Ltd, 1927), 77.

133 Irene Nowell OSB, *Women in the Old Testament*, 52–53.

134 Philip J. Budd, *Numbers* WBC, Vol. 5, 137.

135 Philip J. Budd, *Numbers* WBC, Vol. 5, 137.

136 Ashley R Timothy, *The Book of Numbers*, 227.

137 Martin Noth, *Numbers – A Commentary* (London: SCM Press, 1968), 97.

138 Philip J. Budd, *Numbers* WBC, Vol. 5, 138

139 Gordon J. Wenham, *Numbers: An Introduction and Commentary* (Illinois: InterVarsity Press, 1981), 113.

140 Ashley R. Timothy, *The Book of Numbers*, 228.

141 Philip J. Budd, *Numbers*, 137.

This is done to a girl when she becomes guilty in some shameful way. The same thing is applied to Miriam also. Spitting on the face of Miriam is considered to be a public insult which is part of the penalty. Likewise, exclusion from the community is seen as public shame.[142] It is not only an act of contempt, but it also carries a curse with it.[143]

### Verse 15

The act of waiting by the community ensures the readers that she was accepted as a leader.[144] No information is found about the happenings to Miriam during those seven days.

### Verse 16

This verse depicts the report of occurrences in the journey. There is a comment that v.16 is a part of editorial job.[145]

## 8. Theological Connotations

Milgrom highlights the function of Moses as an intercessor. Moses' successful intercession for Miriam brought down the anger of God. Need for intercession aroused, because of the complaint made by Miriam. The penalization by God ensures that complaints would call for divine judgment.[146]

## 9. General Observations

In the light of textual context, it needs to be understood that people's popular rebellion was based on dissatisfaction about manna which was the daily food available.[147] Since Moses had trouble in handling the people, God instructs Moses to appoint seventy leaders upon whom God's spirit descended.[148] So they have become instruments of

---

142 N. H. Snaith, *Leviticus and Numbers,* 236.

143 Elliott Binns, *The Book of Numbers,* 78.

144 Ashley R. Timothy, *The Book of Numbers,* 228.

145 Elliott Binns, *The Book of Numbers,* 78.

146 Gordon J. Wenham, *Numbers,* 94–99.

147 cf. Numbers 11.

148 Naomi Graetz, "Did Miriam Talk Too Much," 236.

God in handling people. In this context, it is natural to ask whether God speaks only through Moses.

Deen speculates that Zipporah who is the first wife of Moses had died. Hence, Moses married a Cushite (Ethiopian), a dark-skinned woman from the African country bordering on Egypt.[149] But according to Exodus 18:2,[150] Moses had sent her (Zipporah) away.[151] Then Moses married a Cushite woman.[152] Miriam despised the Cushite woman whom Moses married - not because of jealousy, colour, or race but because the Cushite woman was a foreigner. Miriam feared that Moses would be influenced to move away from Yahweh.[153] There is an opinion which regards the Cushite woman as referring to Zipporah, daughter of Jethro.[154] Zipporah was the sixth woman[155] in Moses' story who functions prominently saving the life of Moses. Her act of saving is through circumcision.[156] Zipporah's action was unique and redemptive.[157] After this incident, the biblical tradition takes shows little interest in Zipporah.[158]

Both Miriam and Aaron "spoke against" Moses in connection with the Cushite woman he had married (Numbers 12:1), but what then followed had apparently nothing to do with the Cushite woman. As a result of leprosy, she too has become an outcaste and

149 Edith Deen, *All of the Women of the Bible,* 60.

150 Modern translations say, he divorced her.

151 There is also a possibility that Miriam and Aaron would have objected Moses for divorcing Zipporah. Moreover, after the arrival of Zipporah back to Moses, Aaron and Miriam could have protested on behalf of Zipporah to Moses. If this is so, then their protest is a valid one. This protest could be a protest against rupture of relationship.

152 N. H. Snaith, *Leviticus and Numbers,* 234.

153 Alice L. Laffey, *An Introduction to the Old Testament: A Feminist Perspective,* 53.

154 Edith Deen, *All of the Women of the Bible*, 324.

155 Other five women who saved Moses were, midwives who saved Israelite male babies, mother and sister of Moses, Pharaoh's daughter.

156 cf. Exodus 4: 19 – 26.

157 Irene Nowell OSB, *Women in the Old Testament,* 56–57.

158 Eileen Schulier, "Women of the Exodus in Biblical Retellings of the Second Temple Period," in *Gender and Difference in Ancient Israel,* edited by Peggy L Day (Minneapolis: Fortress Press, 1989), 180.

rejected without voice and power.[159] Yet another pertinent issue that arises is that even though Aaron was also part of confronting Moses, Aaron was not punished. This could be an example of the manner in which a patriarchal society might function. Even though Aaron was not affected, he exhibits his solidarity with Miriam. Brotherly love is being revealed by Moses and Aaron.

## 10. Why was Miriam being punished with leprosy?

Words of Miriam and Aaron were centered on the claim to be leaders and prophets for the Israelites along with Moses. Conceivably, a dispute over the marrying of a Cushite woman might have precipitated a power confrontation. As it has been mentioned, 70 elders have been selected to share the burden of leadership. Moses' statement in Numbers 11.29 ensures that spirit of God has come upon Eldad and Medad who also will be considered to be prophets.[160] According to the Midrash, Miriam committed the sin of slander[161] against Moses. For Rabbis, Aaron is a passive accessory rather than active co-agent.[162] But in relation to Number 12, Aaron and Miriam spoke against Moses. But Miriam alone was punished.[163] When the linguistic tools are employed, it is visible that the verb rBe'd: 'spoke' appears to be in third feminine singular form – "she spoke". Actually it should have appeared in the plural form – "they spoke."[164] It is probable that the Priestly writers wanted to portray Aaron as clean and involved faithfully in ritualistic activities.[165] Because the Book of Leviticus emphasizes that as per regulations, a Priest should be physically unblemished.[166]

---

159 Phyllis Trible, "Bringing Miriam out of the Shadows," 177.

160 Naomi Graetz, "Did Miriam Talk Too Much," 236.

161 In today's context, it is character assassination.

162 Naomi Graetz, "Did Miriam Talk Too Much," 238.

163 Plaut opines that Aaron was mentally punished. It could be explained as, hurt of seeing the dear one suffering is greater than one's own physical agony. Next, Aaron has to humiliate himself by begging Moses for forgiveness.

164 Naomi Graetz, "Did Miriam Talk Too Much," 231.

165 Carol A. Newsom & Sharon H. Ringe, ed., *The Women's Bible Commentary* (London: SPCK, 1992), 47–48.

166 cf. Leviticus 21–22.

Numbers 13 is the story of the 12 spies who go out on a scouting mission to study the land of Canaan, ten of whom come back with slanderous comments about the Land. They are not allowed to enter the Promised Land. This passage could be connected with chapter 12 basing on the connotation of 'slander' against God.[167] This portrays the boldness of Miriam to question a leader for his actions.

## 11. What sort of pain, would Miriam have experienced when she was infected with leprosy?

Miriam would have felt that it is better to die rather than live with leprosy. She felt lonely and abandoned and perhaps felt that she was despised by the community. She would have been depressed thinking of how to reveal to others, that she was innocent, and the real reason why she was infected with leprosy. As common human tendency, she would have desired to be restored to health.

## 12. Emotions of Miriam when she was placed outside the camp?

Miriam's emotions when she was placed outside the camp could be elucidated in physical, psychological and spiritual terms. Physically, she was struck with leprosy and being isolated from the community without any companionship. She might have even wept angrily for her sickness. Psychologically, she should have under gone mental pressure, feeling of self – hatredness, oppression and discrimination. She might have even decided not to mingle and speak with others. Moreover, she might have contemplated whether she will be accepted by her family again or not. Queries and doubts about her healing would have been running in her mind during her stay outside the camp. Spiritually, she would have even questioned God for punishing her with leprosy. She might have had the feeling that she is being rejected by God. Due to frustration, she would have even thought that there is no purpose in living and it is better to commit suicide.

---

167 Naomi Graetz, "Did Miriam Talk Too Much," 236.

## 13. How is this story significant for the AIDS affected woman in India?

Miriam received leprosy because of speaking against God. But a woman living with AIDS received this illness because of unawareness. Miriam's disease is visible to others, but the illness of a woman living with AIDS is not easily visible. When Miriam was affected with leprosy, Moses interceded to God for her healing. But when an individual is asked to pray for the woman living with AIDS, he/she starts to think instead on how she would have infected with this illness. Although, Aaron and Miriam slandered against God, Miriam was alone punished. Similarly, only women are blamed for being affected with HIV and AIDS. Miriam's physical illness has been cured, but still the physical and mental curing of woman living with AIDS has not occurred. They are being excluded by the society and looked on negatively by the communities. Miriam's silence[168] cannot be avoided without notice. She does not speak after this until Numbers 20 where information about her death is mentioned.[169] This silence has semblance with women living with HIV and AIDS who are made silent after being infected with this sickness. Even though they have received it passively, they cannot raise voice against their situation. Physical suffering is present in the lives of woman living with AIDS. It also includes loneliness because of excommunication from family and friends. They are also forced to experience denial of human rights,[170] stigma of pollution. It is evident that, women living with HIV and AIDS are victimized by make judgmental statements like the disease is the consequence of sin.

---

168 No linage, birth announcement or naming ritual proclaims the advent of Miriam. She entered the scripture obliquely. Only silence gives her birth. Phyllis Trible, "Bringing Miriam out of the Shadows, 169.

169 Monica Jyotsna Melanchthon, "Facing HIV and AIDS: Some Insights from the Hebrew Bible," 81.

170 Widow living with AIDS is being thrown out from the husband's family. She has no control over her husband's property. In some cases, even children are being alienated from the mother.

## 14. Does this text have any liberative elements for the AIDS sufferer? If so what are they? What lessons does the text offer to the community/church?

Miriam was punished for speaking against God, but there are many women and children who have not done anything wrong, but affected with AIDS. They should not be excommunicated, rather they should be treated with love, care by society/church. As Aaron confessed that his words were wrong in v.11, church should confess for stigmatizing and labeling woman living with AIDS as sinners.[171]

# 2 Kings 5:8-14

## 15. Translation

### V. 8

וַיְהִי כִּשְׁמֹעַ אֱלִישָׁע אִישׁ־הָאֱלֹהִים כִּי־קָרַע מֶלֶךְ־יִשְׂרָאֵל אֶת־בְּגָדָיו וַיִּשְׁלַח אֶל־הַמֶּלֶךְ לֵאמֹר לָמָּה קָרַעְתָּ בְּגָדֶיךָ יָבֹא־נָא אֵלַי וְיֵדַע כִּי יֵשׁ נָבִיא בְּיִשְׂרָאֵל׃

And it was so when Elisha[172] the man of God[173] heard that the king[174] of Israel had torn his garments, he sent to the king, saying, "Why have you torn your garments? I pray that, let him come to me, and he shall know that there is a prophet[175] in Israel"

### V. 9

וַיָּבֹא נַעֲמָן בְּסוּסוֹ וּבְרִכְבּוֹ וַיַּעֲמֹד פֶּתַח־הַבַּיִת לֶאֱלִישָׁע׃

Then Naaman went with his horse and with his chariot, and stopped at the entrance of the house of Elisha.

171 Woman living with AIDS should not be blamed.

172 אֱלִישָׁע "Elisha" is missing in the Manuscripts of LXX. Perhaps the LXX wants to give importance to God and not to Prophet.

173 אִישׁ־הָאֱלֹהִים "Man of God" is missing in LXX. LXX does not qualify the name 'Elisha' to be the man of God.

174 LXX, Syriac reads it as המלך "The King."

175 Some manuscripts have אֱלֹהִים "God" instead of the word 'Prophet.' Usage of the term "Elohim" has been used to portray the power of God.

## V. 10

וַיִּשְׁלַח אֵלָיו אֱלִישָׁע מַלְאָךְ לֵאמֹר הָלוֹךְ וְרָחַצְתָּ שֶׁבַע־פְּעָמִים בַּיַּרְדֵּן וְיָשֹׁב
בְּשָׂרְךָ לְךָ וּטְהָר׃

And Elisha sent a messenger to him, saying, go and wash seven times in the Jordan, and your flesh shall be turned and you shall be cleansed.

## V. 11

וַיִּקְצֹף נַעֲמָן וַיֵּלַךְ וַיֹּאמֶר הִנֵּה אָמַרְתִּי אֵלַי יֵצֵא יָצוֹא וְעָמַד וְקָרָא
בְּשֵׁם־יְהוָה אֱלֹהָיו וְהֵנִיף יָדוֹ אֶל־הַמָּקוֹם וְאָסַף הַמְּצֹרָע׃

But Namaan was angry and went and said, Behold I said to me, he will surely come out and stand and call by the name of Yahweh his Elohim,[176] and wave his hand over the place, and heal the leprosy.

## V. 12

הֲלֹא טוֹב אֲבָנָה וּפַרְפַּר נַהֲרוֹת דַּמֶּשֶׂק מִכֹּל מֵימֵי יִשְׂרָאֵל הֲלֹא־אֶרְחַץ בָּהֶם
וְטָהָרְתִּי וַיִּפֶן וַיֵּלֶךְ בְּחֵמָה׃

Whether Abanah[177] and Pharpar, rivers of Damascus are not good than all the waters of Israel? Could I not wash[178] in them and be cleaned? Then he turned and walked in rage.

## V. 13

וַיִּגְּשׁוּ עֲבָדָיו וַיְדַבְּרוּ אֵלָיו וַיֹּאמְרוּ אָבִי דָּבָר גָּדוֹל הַנָּבִיא דִּבֶּר אֵלֶיךָ
הֲלוֹא תַעֲשֶׂה וְאַף כִּי־אָמַר אֵלֶיךָ רְחַץ וּטְהָר׃

And his servants came and certainly spoke to him, and said,[179] "My father, if[180] the prophet has spoken to you great, would you have not done? And[181] also that he said, "wash and be cleaned".

---

176 In manuscripts of LXX, יְהוָה "Yahweh" is missing.

177 Multiple manuscripts of Syriac and Targum have אֲמָנָה Amanah. It is the mountain region of the anti-Lebanon.
Mordechai Cogan & Hayim Tadmor, *2 Kings* (USA: Doubleday & Company, 1988), 64.

178 LXX adds πορευθεὶς which means "to go/proceed."

179 וַיֹּאמְרוּ "and they said" is missing in the manuscripts of LXX, Syriac and Vulgate

180 LXX adds εἰ אם 'if'. This addition enables one to look at it as an interrogative.

181 This conjunction 'and' is missing in some of the manuscripts.

## V. 14

וַיֵּ֗רֶד וַיִּטְבֹּ֤ל בַּיַּרְדֵּן֙ שֶׁ֣בַע פְּעָמִ֔ים כִּדְבַ֖ר אִ֣ישׁ הָאֱלֹהִ֑ים וַיָּ֣שָׁב בְּשָׂר֗וֹ כִּבְשַׂ֛ר
נַ֥עַר קָטֹ֖ן וַיִּטְהָֽר׃

So he went down and dipped in the Jordan seven times, according to the speech of the man of God;[182] and his flesh turned like the flesh of the small child, and he was clean.

## 16. Date of Compilation

The date of compilation of the book of Kings is traced to the period of exile. For some, the major part of the compilation was completed in Babylon by an exiled scribe. Probably the book would have reached its present form between 561 and 538.[183]

## 17. Structure

| | |
|---|---|
| The problem and its background | 5:1 – 2 |
| Israelite maid's speech | 5:3 |
| Meeting the King of Aram & King's response | 5:4 – 5 |
| Meeting the King of Israel | 5:6 |
| Israelite King's response | 5:7 |
| Elisha's word to the king | 5:8 |
| Naaman's arrival outside the house of Elisha | 5:9 |
| Elisha's action | 5:10 |
| Naaman's departure with ignorant arrogance complaint | 5:11 – 12 |
| Intervention by Naaman's servant | 5:13 |
| Advice followed and received cure by Naaman | 5:14[184] |

## 18. Genre

Burke is of the opinion that this text belongs to a Prophetic Legendry. It is a story which tries to portray the prophet as a worker of mighty miracles, holder of divine power, exemplar of God-filled piety and

---

182 In LXX, Elisha is only identified by his name and not as the 'man of God'.

183 Theodore H. Robinson, *The Decline and Fall of the Hebrew Kingdoms* (Oxford: Clarendon Press, 1952), 50.

184 Burke O. Long, *2 Kings* (Michigan: William B. Eerdmans Publishing Company, 1991), 66.

morality. Rofe calls this a 'Didactic or Ethical *legendum*'.[185] Eissfeldt identifies this passage as a "historical narrative" because of the presence of two kings in the story. DeVries names it as "power demonstration narrative" that illustrates the activities of the prophet.[186]

## 19. Context

The stories in 2 Kings 2:22 – 5:27 contain a shift from problem to solution. In the preceding chapters, a limited number of main characters appear with lack of characterization. In 2:19 – 22, two main characters which appear are Elisha and the men of the city. In 2:23 – 24, three main characters are Elisha, boys and the bears. In 4:1 – 7, four main characters are Elisha, the widow and her two sons. In 4:8 – 37, the five characters are Elisha, the Shunemite woman, her husband, her son and Gehazi.[187] In 4:38 – 44, Elisha and two sons of the prophet are found. In 5:1 – 27, the story of Naaman, a little less than ten characters appear. As the characters increase, there are several subplots coming out.[188] In this story, Naaman, the higher official is a leper. A captive Israelite maid has pity on her master and suggests that he might be cured by the prophet in Samaria.[189] Naaman carried this suggestion to the king. The King sends a letter to the king of Israel concerning Naaman's sickness. Basically, Israel was a land often at war with Syria and repeatedly defeated by the Syrian armies.[190] This letter was considered to be the plot for a battle. Then the Prophet Elisha is introduced and the solution for leprosy has been announced through a prophet's messenger. By responding to the commandment of the prophet, Naaman received healing. The story continues with the actions of Gehazi.

---

185 Burke O Long, *2 Kings*, 77.

186 R. T. Hobbs, *2 Kings*, WBC, Vol. 13 (Texas: Word Books Publisher, 1985), 58.

187 In the narrative, Elisha has no contact with Shunamite husband.

188 R. T. Hobbs, *2 Kings*, 59.

189 James A. Montgomery, *A Critical and Exegetical Commentary on the Books of Kings* (Edinburgh: T & T Clark, 1976), 374.

190 Ronald S. Wallace, *Elijah and Elisha: Expositions from the Book of Kings* (Edinburgh: Oliver and Boyd, 1957), 129.

## 20. Character study

### 20.1. Naaman

The name 'Naaman' appears in the Ugaritic tablets which explain that Naaman was a higher official in the army of the king of Aram.[191] It was a great shock for Naaman to discover that he had leprosy in the midst of his absorbing life in Syria. Even though Syria gave him birth, food, education and amusement, it could not wash him clean from leprosy. His pride and confidence in Syria was shattered when he started to search for cleansing from his skin ailment. He became humble enough to listen to the wisdom of a little girl than the wise people of Syria.[192]

### 20.2. King of Israel

The name of the king is not mentioned in this passage. But it is presumed to be Jehoram. Jehoram is an idolater for whom Elisha had no respect,[193] but he helps the king during the tragic situation.[194] Jehoram, King of Israel interpreted the request letter as some kind of threat. He reacted as though he encountered deep trouble by tearing his clothes. He also announces his powerlessness using the words "am I God to kill and to make alive?"[195] The King seems to be ineffective without the help of a prophet.[196]

---

191 James A. Montgomery, *A Critical and Exegetical Commentary on the Books of Kings,* 373.

192 Ronald S. Wallace, *Elijah and Elisha: Expositions from the Book of Kings,* 131-133.

193 cf. 2 Kings 3:13 – 14.

194 Laurel Lanner, "Cannibal Mothers and Me: A Mother's Reading of 2 Kings 6.24-7.20" in *Samuel and Kings: A Feminist Companion to the Bible,* edited by Athalya Brenner (England: Sheffield Academic Press, 2000), 132.

195 Burke O. Long, *2 Kings,* 70.

196 Claudia V. Camp, "1 and 2 Kings", in *The Women's Bible Commentary,* edited by Carol A. Newsom and Sharon H. Ringe (Louisville: John Knox Press, 1992), 108.

## 20.3. Elisha

In general, Prophet Elisha was a man of God having an unwavering source of power. He enacted in a role of a magician and wonder worker. He is very useful to the king, by aiding him in his distress.[197] In particular, even though he is introduced as נָבִיא "Prophet", prophetic characteristics are not visible here. There is no mention of traditional prophetic speech formulas as it is found in 1:4, 17; 2:21,22.[198] In this passage, Elisha follows his normal custom of speaking through an intermediary.[199] Feminist scholars critically questioned the chastity of Prophet Elisha by looking at his relationship with the woman at Shunem (2 Kings 4.8 - 37).[200] He is considered by some to be the father for the child born to the woman at Shunem.

## 20.4. Hebrew Girl

The humble Hebrew girl expressed her concern, affirmed her faith. She is an example for someone playing a major role despite being a minor biblical character.[201] von Rad added theological flavor to the life of the little girl by saying that she was an instrument being offered by God to save Naaman.[202] The girl's belief in the power of the prophet to cure Naaman from leprosy is revealed.[203] The nameless maid and the nameless woman (wife of Naaman) played a significant role in the whole story. If these two people were absent, Naaman would have remained a leper. The Israelite maid had faith

---

197 Wesley J. Bergen, *Elisha and the End of Prophetism* (England: Sheffield Academic Press, 1999), 124-127.

198 R. T. Hobbs, *2 Kings*, 58.

199 Raymond Calkins, "The First and Second Books of Kings", in *The Interpreter's Bible*, Vol. 3, edited by George Arthur Buttrick (Nashville: Abingdon Press, 1954), 211.

200 Fokkelien van Dijk-Hemmes, "The Great Woman of Shunem and the Man of God: A Dual Interpretation of 2 Kings 4.8 – 37" in *A Feminist Companion to Samuel and Kings,* edited by Athalya Brenner (England: Sheffield Academic Press, 1994), 225 227.

201 Raymond Calkins, "The First and Second Books of Kings", 210.

202 Gerhard von Rad, "Naaman: A Critical Retelling" in *God at Work in Israel* (Nashville: Abingdon Press, 1980), 48.

203 Wesley J. Bergen, *Elisha and the End of Prophetism,* 114.

in the prophet and proclaimed that faith to her mistress. And the mistress in turn, shared this to her husband.[204]

## 21. Setting

Tale-telling, legends were popular in different societal situations. There is no evidence to claim that legends about prophets are restricted to one particular social group in the ancient story. Depending on the situations and intentions of the author, such stories are transmitted to different people. Naturally this collection could be part of Elisha's traditions. For Elisha, this is the second time[205] that he deals with a non-Israelite. Here, he is presented with an opportunity to encounter Aramean military pressures.[206]

## 22. Comments

### Verse 8

A prophet was expected to bring God's presence through his words and actions.[207] Probably, Elisha was still at Gilgal when Naaman arrived.[208] Elisha sends a note to ensure that he is very much present. Elisha's power as a 'man of God' contrasts with the powerlessness of the unnamed 'man of State'.[209]

### Verse 9

Naaman comes to Elisha's house with all the display of his status. Naaman traveling in chariots indicates that the house of Elisha was situated in a more spacious place. Perhaps, he would have lived in

---

204 Alice L. Laffey, *An Introduction to the Old Testament: A Feminist Perspective* (Philadelphia: Fortress Press, 1988), 136–137.

205 cf. 2 Kings 4:8-37.

206 Burke O Long, *2 Kings,* 78.

207 J. Robinson, *The Second Book of Kings,* CBC (New York: Cambridge University Press, 1987), 54.

208 R. T. Hobbs, *2 Kings*, 64.

209 Donald J. Wiseman, *1 and 2 Kings,* Tyndale Old Testament Commentaries (London: InterVarsity Press, 1993), 207.

an isolated house or in the official quarters and not in the thickly populated normal congested quarters.[210]

## Verse 10

Actually Naaman was expecting a red carpet treatment which would be a performance of dignified and worthy ceremony.[211] But unfortunately, the prophet did not even meet Naaman. He sent his mediator and suggested that Naaman dip in the Jordan River seven times. It has been suggested that the ritual of cleansing in rivers has its origination from primitive worship of river gods in AWA. But none of the semitic gods like Resheph, Enlil, Ishtar are associated with water.[212]

## Verse 11

Naaman expected the prophet to come out personally, greet him, offer solemn prayers and do some dramatic gestures[213] like 'waving his hand' or 'stretching out the rod', etc. וְהֵנִיף יָדוֹ 'Wave his hand' is a rare expression in OT. It is connected with ritual of "waving" offerings before their presentations.[214] But in prophetic literature, this could be a synonym for judgment.[215] The egocentric objection of Naaman is visible in this verse.[216] The Jordan River was prescribed for healing. This river is not pure; it contains muddy water when compared with the cool streams of Damascus.[217] Naaman was depicted to be intransigently arrogant and having a misguided attitude towards Elisha.[218]

---

210 John Gray, *I & II Kings: A Commentary* (London: SCM Press Ltd, 1964), 454.

211 Ronald S. Wallace, *Elijah and Elisha: Expositions from the Book of Kings,* 134.

212 R. T. Hobbs, *2 Kings* WBC, Vol. 13, 64.

213 R. C. Dentan, *I & II Kings, I & II Chronicles* (London: SCM Press Ltd, 1964), 81.

214 cf. Leviticus 14:12

215 R. T. Hobbs, *2 Kings,* 65.

216 Richard D. Nelson, *First and Second Kings: Interpretation – A Bible Commentary for Teaching and Preaching* (Atlanta: John Knox Press, 1987), 178.

217 George Adam Smith, *Historical Geography of the Holy Land* (London: Hodder & Stoughton, 1931), 486.

218 Burke O. Long, *2 Kings,* 69.

## Verse 12

Abanah is identical with Amanah. Amanah is the Syrian Mountain which is named as Ammana. Pharpar is usually identified with *Nahr el-A'waj,* which flows from its source in Mount Hermon to the marshland south-east of Damascus. Its name is still preserved in one of the tributaries of the *Nahr el-A'waj.*[219] Ronald opines that Rivers Abanah and Pharpar rise from the mountains of Lebanon and pours into the land of Damascus. In its journey, it irrigates and makes the land fertile.[220]

## Verse 13

*'my father'* – this is the most irregular form of address by a servant to his master. In general, אֲדֹנִי *'my lord'*[221] is the terminology used by the servants to call the master.[222] His servants cared for him by being very pragmatic.[223] Even though Naaman was powerful and wealthy, he is expected to accept healing by simply washing in the river.[224]

## Verse 14

The verb ירד "went down" denotes more than physical descent. Moore proposes that "Naaman is also descending from his attitude of superiority. He submits to the prophet. The healing took place not because of any magical power in the Jordan River, but because of obedience to Elisha's words.[225] Usage of the verb טָבַל 'to dip' was unusual, because it occurs only 16 times in the whole of the OT. It

219 Roland E. Clements, *1 and 2 Kings,* New Century Bible Commentary (London: Eerdmans Publishing, 1984), 417.

220 Ronald S. Wallace, *Elijah and Elisha: Expositions from the Book of Kings,* 129.

221 Mordechai Cogan & Hayim Tadmor, *2 Kings,* 65.

222 cf. 2 Kings 6:15; Numbers 11:28; Genesis 44:5.

223 Graeme Auld, *I & II Kings* (Philadelphia: Westminister Press, 1986), 168.

224 R. T. Hobbs, *2 Kings,* 65.

225 Ngan Elizabeth Ling Lai, *2 Kings* 5 (Review and Expositor Vol. 94, No.4, Louisville: Review & Expositor Inc. 1997), 589-593.

refers to objects dipped in blood,[226] water,[227] and in other liquids.[228] This verb is not a synonym for washing.[229] כִּבְשַׂר נַעַר קָטֹן וַיִּטְהָר 'like the flesh of the small child, and he was clean' – this statement may remind the reader about the innocent young girl who began Naaman's search for cure.

## 23. Explanation

Israel was in constant battle with Syria for many years. But this chapter deals with the incident of peace which is wrought through healing.[230] Naaman was a leper. The Hebrew term is broadly generic, covering a large variety of scabious diseases.[231] Possibly, it was a skin disease which resulted in whiteness and dryness of the skin tissues.[232] Naaman's "leprosy" was not what is clinically known as leprosy in today's context. It could be a skin ailment which demands exclusion from the community.[233] When the miracles are compared with 2 kings 4, Naaman was expected to learn that there is a prophet in Israel. As a result, this becomes a witness for the status of Elisha as a prophet.[234] By hearing Elisha's instructions, Naaman reacts with anger and pique. Through this, a bundle of habitual attitudes and royal characters are revealed.[235] He did not realize yet the words of the prophet which contains the power of God. But the prophet's words are re-echoed by his servants.[236] By obeying the words of prophet, he received complete healing.

---

226 cf. Leviticus 14:6.

227 cf. 2 Kings 8:15.

228 cf. Deuteronomy 33:24; 1 Samuel 14:27.

229 R. T. Hobbs, *2 Kings*, 65.

230 R. C. Dentan, *I & II Kings, I & II Chronicles*, 80.

231 James A. Montgomery, *A Critical and Exegetical Commentary on the Books of Kings*, 373.

232 R. T. Hobbs, *2 Kings*, 63.

233 Graeme Auld, *I & II Kings*, 167-168.

234 R. T. Hobbs, *2 Kings*, 68.

235 Burke O. Long, *2 Kings*, 71.

236 Alice L. Laffery, *First Kings and Second Kings: Collegeville Bible* Commentary (Mumbai: St. Paul's, 2001), 70-71.

## 24. Theological Connotations

Elisha is presented as the 'Prophet in Samaria' which resulted in teaching Naaman that there is a prophet available in Israel. The name of Yahweh has been introduced in this narration by Naaman. Yahweh has come to the scene as the God of Elisha. As the story goes, Naaman is converted from arrogance to humility. He was healed not due to the cleansing power of the river Jordan, but by simple open-minded obedience. At the end, it forces Naaman to express explicitly his monotheistic confession.[237]

## 25. Why was Naaman seeking to have his leprosy cured?

Naaman was seeking to be cured from his leprosy because he was a commander/captain to the Aram's army. It is interesting that despite his skin ailment he continued to live in his own home. People with leprosy were usually sent away to a leper's colony. Probably, since he was an influential man, he was allowed to stay in a residential area or his skin ailment was not a serious one. In either case, the narrative raises queries about class and illness and it gives the message to its readers that one's class might affect access to healing. This sickness would have stopped him from continuing to work in the army. Since he was highly esteemed by his master and acted as an instrument for the victory to Aram, he had the wherewithal to search for a cure. He could have the interest to go to warfare and fight for his people and rulers, but the sickness hinders his travel to warfare.

## 26. What were Naaman's expectations when he was washing himself in the Jordan River?

Naaman wanted to get well by any means. He would have had the thirst to be cured. He may have wondered about the possibilities of being cured. Even though Naaman was holding a good position in his country, he may have wondered if by dipping himself he was polluting the river Jordan. He probably even considered those people living in the surrounding area of Jordan River and if they would be disturbed by his bath. He could have expected his flesh to become

237 Richard D. Nelson, *First and Second Kings: Interpretation – A Bible Commentary for Teaching and Preaching,* 181-183.

like the flesh of a lad. He might have even thought that Prophet Elisha is making fun at him. Through the hopeful words installed by his servants, he might have had little faith about his healing.

### 27. Since Naaman was infected with leprosy, what problems might he have faced as a captain for the host of King Syria?

Some of the problems that Naaman faced could be humiliation, maltreatment, being insulted, mentally disturbed, shame, inferiority complex, frustrated, use of harmful words against his actions by officials. He might have received disobedience from soldiers. Some would have seen him with disgust. It might not have been possible for him to go to his work regularly and enjoy full freedom to execute his work.

### 28. How is this Story significant for AIDS affected woman in India?

Women mentioned in this story are nameless heroines who were not credited for their contribution. But in Indian scenario, even if HIV and AIDS is contracted through the husband, the wife is blamed. Next, Naaman was able to bear all the troubles that he encountered in the midst of adversities. By obeying the words of Elisha, Naaman received peace and harmony in life. When these stories of suffering are read from the Bible with heart and mind, it gives space to relate oneself with the sufferers which might give some kind of consolation to the readers. Naaman did not encounter assault in his work spot. Whereas, when a woman is affected with HIV, she becomes jobless. She does not receive love or care, but investigation is made about the mode of infection of HIV. Her character and behavior is questioned. Like Naaman experienced shame, so too, women living with HIV and AIDS are not comfortable to share their health status with others. Naaman may not have been comfortable to go to war field to fight the battle, but women living with HIV and AIDS could enjoy the freedom of moving and mingling with the community.[238]

238 But in reality, this freedom is not enjoyed by all women living with HIV and AIDS.

## 29. Does this text have any liberative elements for the AIDS sufferer? If so what are they? What lessons does the text offer to the community/church?

As Naaman obeyed and took a bath in the Jordan River, medicines should be consumed by AIDS sufferer as prescribed by doctors. Since AIDS is not a contagious disease, human relationships can be strengthened among human beings. As Elisha identified the real problem of Naaman and cared for it, the church needs to pay attention to the suffering community and exhibit love and concern towards them. This would surely enhance the life and position of women living with HIV and AIDS.

# Ezekiel 37:1-14

## 30. Translation

### V. 1

הָיְתָה עָלַי יַד־יְהוָה וַיּוֹצִאֵנִי בְרוּחַ יְהוָה וַיְנִיחֵנִי בְּתוֹךְ הַבִּקְעָה וְהִיא מְלֵאָה עֲצָמוֹת׃

The hand of Yahweh came[239] upon me, and He brought me out in the Spirit of Yahweh[240] and set me down in the midst of the valley; and it was full of human bones.[241]

239 הָיְתָה – The Septuagint and The Syriac version of the OT has - καὶ ἐγένετο, which means 'and it came or became.' Since this verse is the beginning of a new chapter, there is no need to mention it. So, the Masoretic text can be retained.

240 בְרוּחַ יְהוָה – Literally, "the Spirit of God," apparently used as a stereotyped term in this clause where the LORD is subject.

241 עֲצָמוֹת – The Septuagint and The Targum(s) adds ἀνθρωπίνων, which indicates the 'human bones.' The text can be amended for purposes of clarity.

## V. 2

וְהֶעֱבִירַ֥נִי עֲלֵיהֶ֖ם סָבִ֣יב ׀ סָבִ֑יב וְהִנֵּ֨ה רַבּ֥וֹת מְאֹד֙ עַל־פְּנֵ֣י הַבִּקְעָ֔ה וְהִנֵּ֖ה יְבֵשׁ֥וֹת מְאֹֽד׃

And He caused me to pass all around[242] among them, and behold,[243] there were a great many on the surface of the valley; and behold, they were very dry.

## V. 3

וַיֹּ֣אמֶר אֵלַ֔י בֶּן־אָדָ֕ם הֲתִֽחְיֶ֖ינָה הָעֲצָמ֣וֹת הָאֵ֑לֶּה וָאֹמַ֕ר אדֹנָ֥י יְהוִ֖ה אַתָּ֥ה יָדָֽעְתָּ׃

And He said to me, "Son of man, can these bones live?" And I answered, "O Adonai[244] Yahweh, you know."

## V. 4

וַיֹּ֣אמֶר אֵלַ֔י הִנָּבֵ֖א עַל־הָעֲצָמ֣וֹת הָאֵ֑לֶּה וְאָמַרְתָּ֣ אֲלֵיהֶ֗ם הָעֲצָמוֹת֙ הַיְבֵשׁ֔וֹת שִׁמְע֖וּ דְּבַר־יְהוָֽה׃

Then He said to me,[245] Son of man, Prophesy over these bones, and say to them, 'O dry bones, hear the word of Yahweh.'

---

242 וְהֶעֱבִירַ֥נִי עֲלֵיהֶ֖ם סָבִ֣יב ׀ סָבִ֑יב - The literal meaning is 'and he made me pass over them, around.' But in the Masoretic text, the grammatical construction is given importance rather than the literal meaning.

243 הִנֵּה – The word הִנֵּה (*hinneh*, traditionally 'behold') indicates becoming aware of something and is here translated as "I realized" because it results from Ezekiel's recognition of the situation around him. In Hebrew, the exclamation is repeated in the following sentence.

244 אדֹנָ֥י – in the Septuagint 'Adonai,' meaning – 'Lord' is deleted. The Masoretic text can be retained.

245 בֶּן־אָדָ֕ם - in some Manuscripts of the Hebrew OT and the Septuagint – 'Son of man,' is added. The text should be amended to beautify this verse.

## V. 5

כֹּה אָמַר אֲדֹנָי יְהוִה לָעֲצָמוֹת הָאֵלֶּה הִנֵּה אֲנִי מֵבִיא בָכֶם
רוּחַ וִחְיִיתֶם׃

"Thus says Adonai[246] Yahweh to these bones, Behold, I will cause breath to enter you[247] that you may come to life."[248]

## V. 6

וְנָתַתִּי עֲלֵיכֶם גִּדִים וְהַעֲלֵתִי עֲלֵיכֶם בָּשָׂר וְקָרַמְתִּי עֲלֵיכֶם עוֹר וְנָתַתִּי
בָכֶם רוּחַ וִחְיִיתֶם וִידַעְתֶּם כִּי־אֲנִי יְהוָה׃

'And I will put sinews on you, and make flesh grow back on you, and cover you with skin, and I will put breath[249] in you that you may come alive; and you will know that I am Yahweh.'

## V. 7

וְנִבֵּאתִי כַּאֲשֶׁר צֻוֵּיתִי וַיְהִי־קוֹל כְּהִנָּבְאִי וְהִנֵּה־רַעַשׁ וַתִּקְרְבוּ עֲצָמוֹת עֶצֶם
אֶל־עַצְמוֹ׃

So, I prophesied as I was commanded;[250] and as I prophesied, there was a noise,[251] and behold, a rattling; and the bones[252] came together, bone to its bone.

---

246 אֲדֹנָי – One of the Hebrew OT and The Septuagint deletes 'Adonai,' meaning – 'Lord.' The Masoretic text can be retained.

247 אֲנִי מֵבִיא בָכֶם רוּחַ – The literal meaning is 'I am about to bring a spirit to you.' In this section רוּחַ variously means "spirit," "breath" and "wind."

248 The Septuagint mentions ζωῆς (noun genitive feminine singular common from ζωη) to indicate the 'life.' The text can be amended to make a more meaningful translation.

249 רוּחַ – The Septuagint mentions μου (pronoun personal genitive singular from ἐγω – its use often serves to emphasize the first person of a verb).

250 צֻוֵּיתִי – in some Manuscripts of the Hebrew OT and the Septuagint, the Syriac version of the OT and the Vulgate has צִוַּנִי (Piel form instead of Pual צֻוֵּיתִי). The Masoretic text can be retained.

251 וַיְהִי־קוֹל – one of the Manuscript of the OT the Septuagint perhaps deletes.

252 עֲצָמוֹת – Two Manuscripts of the Hebrew OT lack it, but perhaps two Medieval Manuscripts of the Hebrew OT, the Septuagint has הָעֲצָמוֹת meaning, "the bones."

## V. 8

וְרָאִיתִי וְהִנֵּה־עֲלֵיהֶם גִּדִים וּבָשָׂר עָלָה וַיִּקְרַם עֲלֵיהֶם עוֹר מִלְמָעְלָה וְרוּחַ
אֵין בָּהֶם׃

And I looked, and behold, sinews were spread[253] on them, and flesh grew, and skin covered over them; but there was no breath in them.

## V. 9

וַיֹּאמֶר אֵלַי הִנָּבֵא אֶל־הָרוּחַ הִנָּבֵא בֶן־אָדָם וְאָמַרְתָּ אֶל־הָרוּחַ כֹּה־אָמַר ׀
אֲדֹנָי יְהוִה מֵאַרְבַּע רוּחוֹת בֹּאִי הָרוּחַ וּפְחִי בַּהֲרוּגִים הָאֵלֶּה וְיִחְיוּ׃

Then He said to me, Prophesy to the breath, prophesy - son of man, and say to the breath, Thus says Adonai[254] Yahweh, "Come from the four winds, O breath,[255] and breathe on these corpses so that they may live."

## V. 10

וְהִנַּבֵּאתִי כַּאֲשֶׁר צִוָּנִי וַתָּבוֹא בָהֶם הָרוּחַ וַיִּחְיוּ וַיַּעַמְדוּ עַל־רַגְלֵיהֶם חַיִל
גָּדוֹל מְאֹד־מְאֹד׃

So I prophesied[256] as He commanded me, and the breath came into them, and they came to life, and stood on their feet, an exceedingly great army.

---

253 וַיִּקְרַם - it is probably read as וַיִּקָּרֵם, (the transitive use in v.6 leads one to expect here a Niphal form) which is compared with the Septuagint, the Syriac Version of the Hebrew OT and the Vulgate.

254 אֲדֹנָי – it is absent in the Septuagint.

255 הָרוּחַ – it is absent in the Septuagint.

256 וְהִנַּבֵּאתִי - some Manuscript has וְהִתְנַבֵּאתִי (the Hithpael form replaces the Niphal used in v.7). Its rare and special usage elsewhere in Ezekiel (13:17) may suggest an error under the influence of the Niphal imperative. It has been proposed to use וְנִבֵּאתִי

## V. 11

וַיֹּאמֶר אֵלַי בֶּן־אָדָם הָעֲצָמוֹת הָאֵלֶּה כָּל־בֵּית יִשְׂרָאֵל הֵמָּה הִנֵּה אמְרִים
יָבְשׁוּ עַצְמוֹתֵינוּ וְאָבְדָה תִקְוָתֵנוּ נִגְזַרְנוּ לָנוּ׃

Then He said to me, Son of man, these bones are the whole house of Israel; behold,[257] they say, 'Our bones are dried up, and our hope has perished.[258] We have been cut off.'[259]

## V. 12

לָכֵן הִנָּבֵא וְאָמַרְתָּ אֲלֵיהֶם כֹּה־אָמַר אֲדֹנָי יְהוִה הִנֵּה אֲנִי פֹתֵחַ
את־קִבְרוֹתֵיכֶם וְהַעֲלֵיתִי אֶתְכֶם מִקִּבְרוֹתֵיכֶם עַמִּי וְהֵבֵאתִי אֶתְכֶם
אֶל־אַדְמַת יִשְׂרָאֵל׃

Therefore prophesy, and say to them,[260] 'Thus says the Adonai[261] Yahweh, Behold, I am about to open your graves and will raise you from your graves, my people;[262] and I will bring you to the land of Israel.'

---

257 הִנֵּה – some Manuscript of the OT has – וְהִנֵּה, which means 'and behold.' The Septuagint uses - καὶ αυτοι, the Targum(s) uses – *h'nwn*, and the Vulgate uses – *ipsi*. The supplying of a pronoun in these texts is a natural clarification of the translators. It is suggested probably to read וְהִנָּם

258 וְאָבְדָה - it is suggested to read with the multiple Manuscripts of the OT, the Septuagint and the Targum(s) has - אָבְדָה. In view of the asyndeton of the next clause the copula in Masoretic Text וְאָבְדָה "and…has perished" is generally deleted as a dittograph in these texts.

259 נִגְזַרְנוּ לָנוּ – it has been proposed to use נִגְזַר נוּלֵנוּ, means "our web is cut off." The Masoretic text can be retained.

260 אֲלֵיהֶם – this is absent in one of the Manuscript, the Septuagint.

261 אֲדֹנָי – it is absent in the Septuagint, but the Masoretic Text adds.

262 עַמִּי - the Masoretic Texts adds עַמִּי "my people," which is unrepresented in the Septuagint and the Syriac Version of the OT and if authentic, expected earlier in the direct speech. It probably originated as a comparative gloss on לעם "to a people" in the verbal covenant formulation of v.27.

## V. 13

וִֽידַעְתֶּ֖ם כִּֽי־אֲנִ֣י יְהוָ֑ה בְּפִתְחִ֣י אֶת־קִבְרֽוֹתֵיכֶ֗ם וּבְהַעֲלוֹתִ֥י אֶתְכֶ֛ם מִקִּבְרוֹתֵיכֶ֖ם
עַמִּֽי׃

Then you will know that I am Yahweh, when I have opened your graves and raise you from your graves, my people.[263]

## V. 14

וְנָתַתִּ֨י רוּחִ֤י בָכֶם֙ וִחְיִיתֶ֔ם וְהִנַּחְתִּ֥י אֶתְכֶ֖ם עַל־אַדְמַתְכֶ֑ם וִֽידַעְתֶּ֞ם כִּֽי־אֲנִ֧י
יְהוָ֛ה דִּבַּ֥רְתִּי וְעָשִׂ֖יתִי נְאֻם־יְהוָֽה׃

And I will put My Spirit within you, and you will come to life, and I will place you on your own land. Then you will know that I am Yahweh, I have spoken and done it, declares Yahweh.

## 31. Date and Time

The book of Ezekiel exemplifies a response to the events of the beginning of the sixth century B.C.E.[264] The statements in the book of Ezekiel which one may regard as reliable (1:1 - 3; 29:17) place the prophet's period of activity between 594 and 571 B.C.E.[265] Jerusalem fell in 586 B.C.E and many of its citizens were taken as captives. As a result of this captivity, Judah lost its temple and it is no longer ruled by a king who belongs to the house of David. Religious life was also not given importance. King, temple and independence were considered as essential for the nation. But as a nation, they lost all the essential things including land. [266] They no longer had a place where they belonged.

## 32. Structure

The message reception formula which usually begins a literary unit, and which will return in v. 15, is here replaced by a formulaic

---

263 עַמִּי - it is absent in the Syriac Version of the OT. In Masoretic Text עַמִּי "my people" has been repeated by dittography from v.12.

264 Henry McKeating, *Ezekiel*, in Old Testament Guides, edited by R. N. Whybray (England: JSOT Press, 1993), 74.

265 Walther Eichrodt, *Ezekiel: A Commentary* (Philadelphia: The Westminster Press, 1970), 1.

266 Henry McKeating, *Ezekiel*, 75.

introduction to a vision account (cf. 1:3; 40:1).[267] The unit of vv. 1-14 continues the vision account of vv. 1-10 with an interpretative oracle of salvation in vv. 11-14. The structure of this text is as follows:

| | |
|---|---|
| Introduction | 37:1a |
| A negative description | 37:1b-2, 8b |
| Divine speech | 37:3, 4, 6, 9, 12 |
| Announcement of divine activity and the positive fulfillment | 37:2, 5, 7, 8 |
| Prophetic transmission | 37:7a, 10a |
| Positive description | 37:7b-8a, 10b |
| Vision account | 37:11-13 |
| Redactional statement | 37:14 |

## 33. Literary Context

Akoto attributes that this passage is supposed to be part of the Qumran texts.[268] This unit reflects a situation filled with hopelessness and shock after the fall of Jerusalem. This kind of situation was quite common during the dissolution of Judah. [269] In the vision account, there is an oracle of disputation. This vision is the exhibition of a field which is filled with scattered and unburied bones in a cemetery. Beentjes calls this to be the prophetical activity of dirge[270] which became an appropriate medium of proclamation to bring life.[271]

267 Leslie C. Allen, *Ezekiel 20 - 48* WBC, Vol. 29 (Texas: Word Books Publisher, 1990), 183.

268 Dorothy Bea Akoto, "Can These Bones Live? Re-reading Ezekiel 37:1-14 in the HIV/AIDS Context," in *Grant me Justice! HIV/AIDS & Gender Readings of the Bible*, Edited by Musa W. Dube and Musimbi R. A. Kanyoro (South Africa: Cluster Publications, 2004), 101.

269 Leslie C. Allen, *Ezekiel 20-48*, 184.

270 Probably, this could mean 'funeral song.'

271 Panc C. Beentjes, "What a Lioness was your Mother - Reflections on Ezekiel 19," in *On Reading Prophetic Texts: Gender-Specific and Related Studies in Memory of Fokkelien van Dijk-Hemmes,* edited by Bob Becking and Meindert Dijkstra (New York: E. J. Brill, 1996), 22-23.

Zimmerli recognizes the relationship between vv.1-10 and 11-14 as that of image and interpretation.[272]

## 34. Explanation

This section represents an autobiographical account of Ezekiel's seizure and commissioning by Yahweh.[273] In terms of traditional history one must look back to Israel's hymnic language which celebrated Yahweh as one who can "kill and make alive."[274] In the Israel's hymnic language, Yahweh is portrayed as one who can "kill and make alive". This is visible in traditional history. Immediate context in 'I wound and heal' and the usage in 2 Kings 5:7, depicts that there is a clear reference to the impression of death which surrounds the victim crisis during the time of illness.[275] 'I wound and heal' - this creedal statement seems to underlie the message of vision and interpretation. The Judeans underwent exile, estranging from both Yahweh and from their land and they were in the status of bewilderment. The prophet proclaims that Yahweh's own desire was to put the people back on their feet. The nation was shown that what looked like a host of skeletons would be turned into an effective army through the power of God's Spirit. This symbolizes that Israel would be restored to life again and filled with the spirit.[276] Ezekiel 37: 24 – 28 reveals a time of rejection being overcome by affirming.[277] The motif of the vision, רוּחַ וִחְיִיתֶם / וְיִחְיוּ "breath, and you may come alive/they may live" loudly proclaims Yahweh to be the creator of new life. Zimmerli comments on the dualistic understanding of

272 Daniel I. Block, *The Book of Ezekiel* NICOT, edited by R. K. Harrison and Robert L. Hubbard (Michigan: Eerdmans, 1998), 371.

273 Daniel I. Block, *The Book of Ezekiel*, 372.

274 cf. Deuteronomy 32:39; 1 Samuel 2:6.

275 Leslie C. Allen, *Ezekiel 20-48*, 187.

276 John B. Taylor, *Ezekiel: An Introduction and Commentary* (Leicester: InterVarsity Press, 1969), 234.

277 Monica J. Melanchthon, *Rejection by God: The History and Significance of the Rejection Motif in the Hebrew Bible* (New York: Peter Lang Publishing Inc, 2001), 5.

human beings.[278] He is of the opinion that the prophet distinguishes between the body, which can be seen with the eyes and felt with the hands, and the life force, which animates the body. But this could be discerned in the breath.[279] Before the exile the temple courts had echoed with personal testimonies of thanksgiving to Yahweh: "For you have delivered my soul from death, my eyes from tears, my feet from stumbling. I walk before the LORD in the land of the living."[280] This cultic legacy was the fuel for an affirmative answer to the lament of the exiles. It provided the theological dynamic for the vision of miraculous renewal. Ezekiel has historicized the Psalms' gospel of reorientation and actualized "the land of the living" sought by the disoriented spreader of lament.[281]

A recurring element in the vision is the prominent role played by Ezekiel as an agent of renewal. He functions not merely as observer but as participant. The vision affirms the reality of divine judgment: Yahweh had indeed dealt a death blow to his covenant people (הרוּגִים – "kill" in v.9; the verb is used of Yahweh's judgment of Israel in 9:6; 21:16; 23:10, 47).[282] However, even from this authentic Sheol the promise of deliverance could be given.

The bones were very dry. The return from exile was no true than a national state which is visible in Ezra and Nehemiah. There was no time, not even under the short-lived Hashmonean rule (140-63 B.C.E.), when anything like a majority of Jews was living in Palestine.[283] The skill used in describing God's work in vv.12 - 14 resting on the ambiguity of רוּחַ. God's breath or spirit must be upon them so that they may return to their land (v.14). Ezekiel had included Israel with Judah in his symbol of the exile (4:4 -6), and now he foretells that they will be united in restoration: he must have

278 Dualistic understanding contrasts "a creaturely body which is from below" with "an immortal soul which is from above."

279 W. Zimmerli, *Ezekiel 2: A Commentary on the Book of the Prophet Ezekiel* (Philadelphia: Fortress Press, 1983), 261.

280 cf. Psalm 116:8-9.

281 Leslie C. Allen, *Ezekiel 20-48,* 188.

282 Leslie C. Allen, *Ezekiel 20-48,* 184.

283 H. L. Ellison, *Ezekiel: The Man and His Message* (Michigan: Eerdmans, 1956), 131.

known of exiles from the Northern Kingdom, who had been carried to Assyria after 722 B.C.E.[284] Yahweh will gather them with their Judaean kinsfolk, into one nation on the mountains of Israel; and one king shall be king to them all.[285]

## 35. Comments

### Verse 1a

The introduction to the vision excitingly describes the psychic experience of being caught up by supernatural power. Divine agency is indicated both by the pressure of Yahweh's "hand" and by the participation of his "spirit."[286] As per the vision, the prophet is being carried away and deposited in a valley.[287] In any event, it is not necessary to think of ecstatic transport as at 8:3; 11: 24, since the prophet is already in Babylonia.[288] The "plain" or broad valley appears to be that mentioned in 3:22-23 and 8:4, close to Ezekiel's residence in the exile at Tel-abib.[289]

### Verses 1b - 3

The visionary scene, a dreadful one, is gradually unfolded. First impressions of a grotesque mass of bones are reinforced as the prophet is taken round the site. He is made aware that once corpses were now rotten or being eaten away into fleshless bones.[290] The divine question is a standard element in a vision, to extract significance from the sight.[291] However, the fact that the question comes from God, the God who kills and makes alive (Deuteronomy 32:39), is enough

284 G. A. Cooke, *The Book of Ezekiel* (Edinburgh: T &T Clark, 1951), 397.

285 G. A. Cooke, *The Book of Ezekiel*, 397-398.

286 cf. Ezekiel 8:3; 11:1, 24.

287 Daniel I. Block, *The Book of Ezekiel*, 373.

288 John W. Wevers, ed., *Ezekiel* (London: Thomas Nelson and Sons Ltd., 1969), 277.

289 Katheryn Pfisterer Darr, "Ezekiel", in *The Women's Bible Commentary*, edited by Carol A. Newsom and Sharon H. Ringe (Louisville: Westminster John Knox Press, 1992), 183.

290 Leslie C. Allen, *Ezekiel 20 - 48*, 185.

291 cf. Jeremiah 1:11, 13; Amos 7:8; 8:2; Zechariah 4:2, 5.

to make Ezekiel guarded about his answer. He had the knowledge not to deny God's ability, but he lacked the faith to believe in it.[292] A seeming corpse might be revived, but these pathetic piles of bones were hopelessly dead. It is obvious that the possibility of a revival did not occur to the prophet; at the time there was no established belief in a resurrection of the dead.[293] So, the prophet's answer shows no hint of a belief in a resurrection, but he realizes that Yahweh is the author of life. Therefore, the divine possibility is left open.[294]

## Verses 4 - 6

Evidently Yahweh knew more than Ezekiel did, for he commands the prophet to address the defunct bones around him and to announce their imminent reanimation. "These bones will live" it is the promise made. The bones are the disjointed, discouraged, dried-out, dismantled house of Israel.[295] This explicates the promise of v.5 in accordance with the 'J' creation story in Genesis 2:7.[296] The resurrection will be in two stages; first complete bodies are formed,[297] and then the bodies are to be animated with breath.[298] Yahweh is portrayed as the creator of the individual, the giver of personal life (cf. Job 10:11-12; Psalm 139:13-16). In the context of restoring life, again Yahweh only bestows it.[299]

## Verses 7 - 8a

The prophetic oracle triggers a movement from disorientation to reorientation. Ezekiel discharges his strange commission, and the ensuing silence is broken by a rattling sound as the bones realign themselves into skeletons. Perhaps noise was introduced as a gloss on shaking. As it is suggested in 3:12 - 13, when both the words

292 John B. Taylor, *Ezekiel: An Introduction and Commentary*, 237.

293 G. A. Cooke, *The Book of Ezekiel*, 399.

294 John W. Wevers, ed., *Ezekiel*, 278.

295 Stuart Briscoe, *Dry Bones* (USA: Victor Books, 1977), 124.

296 John W. Wevers, ed., *Ezekiel*, 278.

297 With sinews, flesh and skin.

298 John W. Wevers, ed., *Ezekiel*, 278.

299 Leslie C. Allen, *Ezekiel 20 - 48*, 185.

occur together, the word may mean an earthquake, sent by God to accompany the prophet's speech.[300] The coming of bones together is not by their own action but by the earthquake shaking that follows on the prophetic word.[301] Then before his wondering eyes they turn into bodies, in step with the stages of his oracle. As in the account of how the first man was made, this leads to the production of complete human forms, but without as yet bringing them to life. God must, once again, breathe in the breath of life, before they can really be brought back to life on earth.[302]

## Verse 8b

However, the narrative lapses into negative description. The process is halted without the emphasized reanimation of vv.5b and 6a having yet taken place. These bodies lack the essential element of "breath," and it requires a further oracle to achieve the renewal of life. Here, separate acts take place because two miracles were necessary, to reconstitute the bones into bodies and to reanimate the bodies.[303]

## Verse 9

The prophetic commission follows the pattern of v.4, but this oracle is to be addressed to the רוּחַ "breath, spirit" that is out there in the wide world. It is summoned from the four quarters of the globe to breathe into the bodies, and thus to animate the whole people. In contrast to Gen.2 the source of the breath of life is the four winds; these signify the four directions, thus the ends of the earth, Ezekiel 42:20;[304] and post-exilic use of the idiom[305] in Zechariah 2:16; 6:5; 1 Chronicles 9:24; Daniel 8:8; 11:4; though it goes back to an Akkadian idiom.[306] The in-breathing echoes the verb of Genesis 2:7

300 G. A. Cooke, *The Book of Ezekiel* (Edinburgh: T &T Clark, 1951), 399.

301 H. L. Ellison, *Ezekiel: The Man and His Message* (Michigan: Eerdmans, 1956), 131.

302 Walther Eichrodt, *Ezekiel: A Commentary* (Philadelphia: The Westminster John Knox Press, 1970), 508.

303 Leslie C. Allen, *Ezekiel 20-48*, 185.

304 cf. Jerermiah. 49:36; 52:23.

305 John W. Wevers, ed., *Ezekiel,* 279.

306 G. A. Cooke, *The Book of Ezekiel,* 400.

(נפח), when Yahweh "breathed" into human being the breath of life. However, the conception seems to be borrowed from 'P' account of creation, in which the term רוּחַ of God floated over the raw elements of the world, waiting to transform them into a living cosmos (Genesis 1:2). It was this pervading power that gave continued life to a finite world (Psalm 104: 29-30; Job 34:14-15).[307]

## Verse 10

Again the prophet functions as an agent of the process, and at last the coming of the breath forecasted in v.5b is achieved. The Hithpael form is elsewhere used in the book only at 13:17, where it characterizes a misused psychic gift of mediating life or death.[308] The superlatives of the negative description in v.2b (מְאֹד -"very," twice) are gathered together in a positive account of the dynamic continuation (מְאֹד, מאד.), to enhance the transformation of bones on an old battlefield into a virile company standing up and so poised and powerful.[309] The contrast is accentuated by the consonantal wordplay between (בּ)הֲרוּגִים הָאֵלֶּה - "these corpses,"[310] referring to the inanimate bodies which the bones had been transformed, and עַל־רַגְלֵיהֶם "on their feet." Furthermore, the notion of new life (יִחְיוּ - "and they became alive") is carried forward in the term חַיִל "army, strength."[311]

## Verse 11

Once more the prophet hears the divine voice, as especially in v.3 and also in vv.4 & 9. The negative factors of vv.1b-2 and 8b are perpetuated in the explanation. The bones represented the exiles, and dramatized the evidence of their own mouths in a communal lament.[312] But G. A. Cooke suggests that the vision explained not

307 Leslie C. Allen, *Ezekiel 20-48*, 185.

308 cf. Ezekiel 13:19.

309 Leslie C. Allen, *Ezekiel 20-48*, 186.

310 cf. Ezekiel 37: 9.

311 Leslie C. Allen, *Ezekiel 20-48*, 186.

312 cf. Ezekiel 33:10.

merely the Judaean exiles, but the entire nation.[313] Their "bones" stand for the whole person, which has been exhausted of vitality by the crisis of exile.[314] All the three expressions signify the death of the nation. The first undoubtedly gave rise to the vision itself. The second is literally 'our hope has perished'.[315] The third is well illustrated in Isaiah 53:8, 'cut off from the land of the living,' which is being meant here.[316] By confessing that "our bones are dried up", there is a notion that exiles were dead both physically[317] and spiritually.[318] This results in ultimate loss of hope and devastation.[319] Their nation had been divided into two kingdoms, and each kingdom had been destroyed. There were fragments of what had been the Hebrew people in Babylon, Egypt, and doubtless in other countries, but the faith and hope embodied in Israel were dead.[320]

## Verses 12 - 13

The divine response to the lament is to commission an oracle of salvation, with opening formulas that deliberately echo those of vv.4-5. In the laments the sensation of death that surrounds the sufferer may be described at one and the same time in terms of drowning and of being caught in a hunter's trap.[321] Mention of the grave finds a parallel in Psalm 88:6, along with the verb "cut off," so that v.12 follows on naturally from the end of v.11. The graves are meant figuratively.[322] The graves suggest the various lands in

313 G. A. Cooke, *The Book of Ezekiel,* 400.

314 cf. Psalm 31:11; 32:3; 102:46.

315 cf. Ezekiel 19:5.

316 John W. Wevers, ed., *Ezekiel,* 279.

317 Several people have died through many battles that they had fought.

318 People's Temple had been destroyed.

319 Dorothy BEA Akoto, "Can These Bones Live? Re-reading Ezekiel 37:1 – 14 in the HIV/AIDS Context," 99.

320 Andrew W. Blackwood, *Ezekiel: Prophecy of Hope* (Michigan: Bakers Book House, 1965), 224.

321 cf. Psalm 18:5-6.

322 G. A. Cooke, *The Book of Ezekiel,* 400.

which the remnant was scattered.[323] Though an actual resurrection of the dead is not implied, the language may have influenced Job 14:11-14; 19:25. The experience of exile is a veritable graveyard; to live again is to return to the land. So, the reference is, not to a physical resurrection, but to a restoration to political existence, as the last clause intimates.[324] The lament is countered with an oracle of salvation that proclaimed afresh the truth of a new Exodus, here expressed in contextually adapted terms, and of a return to the land that symbolized return to living fellowship with Yahweh.[325]

## Verse 14

The vision and its interpretation were of a piece with the message of 36:27, "I will put my spirit upon you," which follows the promise with an assurance of dwelling or settling in the land both in 36:28 and here confirms that an echo of 36:27 is intended.[326] Israel's restoration lies beyond human power, but not beyond the power of God. It is the climatic moment of self-revelation of God.[327] Here are some sequences of promised events. First, "you will come to life" which means before the physical restoration there must be a renewal of faith. Second, "I will place you on your own land" which means the physical restoration will take place. Third, "then you will know that I am God, I have spoken and done it."[328] The metaphorical reviving breath given by Yahweh (v.6) is related to a new potential, the opportunity to comply with Yahweh's covenant terms and used so to enjoy the life.[329] The prophetic experience itself contained seeds of hope for the people of God. The vision's sequence of divine word and action would not fail to have its counterpart in coming reality.[330]

---

323 Andrew W. Blackwood, *Ezekiel: Prophecy of Hope,* 224.

324 John W. Wevers, ed., *Ezekiel,* 279.

325 Leslie C. Allen, *Ezekiel 20-48*, 185.

326 Leslie C. Allen, *Ezekiel 20-48*, 185.

327 Daniel I. Block, *The Book of Ezekiel,* 383.

328 Andrew W. Blackwood, *Ezekiel: Prophecy of Hope,* 224-225.

329 cf. Ezekiel 20:21; 33:19.

330 Leslie C. Allen, *Ezekiel 20-48*, 185.

## 36. Theological Connotations

As in his earlier representations of the netherworld, Ezekiel's vision of the resuscitated dry bones offers his compatriots powerful declarations of hope. The gospel according to Ezekiel affirms that there is life after death, and there is hope beyond grave. Yahweh remains the incontestable Lord not only of the living but also of the dead. The vision of the resuscitation of dry bones is not only for the nation of Israel. The valley represents the whole world, and the bones are the entire human race under the curse of death for its rebellion against God.[331] One theological statement that could be evolved from the text is that, God is faithful and willing to restore the covenant even though humankind violates or breaks the covenantal relationship.[332] "Our bones are dried and our hope is perished" – this lament is met with Yahweh's hopeful response.[333] Accordingly, this text holds out hope for all who accept the grace of God in Christ (Ephesians 2:1-10). With good reason, we who are heirs of the glorious message of the prophets and apostles may find in this text a dramatic affirmation that the sting of death will be overcome by the animating power of Yahweh's Spirit.[334]

## 37. General Observations

The text raises questions about burial practices. The answer could be traced in covenant curses. The practice of throwing bodies out into the open to be eaten by wild animals was present in ancient times. This treatment was applied to those who had broken contracts and treaty oaths. This has been illustrated in Esarhaddon's vassal

---

331 Daniel I. Block, *The Book of Ezekiel: Chapters 25-48* (Michigan: Eerdmans, 1997), 392.

332 Carol J. Dempsey, "The 'Whore' of Ezekiel 16: The Impact and Ramifications of Gender-Specific Metaphors in Light of Biblical Law and Divine Judgment," in *Gender and Law in the Hebrew Bible and the Ancient Near East,* edited by Victor H. Matthews, Bernard M. Levinson and Tikva Frymer-Kensky (England: Sheffield Academic Press Ltd, 1998), 76-77.

333 Dorothy BEA Akoto, "Can These Bones Live? Re-reading Ezekiel 37:1-14 in the HIV/AIDS Context," 100-101.

334 Daniel I. Block, *The Book of Ezekiel,* 392.

treaty.[335] There is no mention about any marauding birds and beasts in this section.[336] Here, the bones on the surface of the valley do not represent just any victims of Nebuchadnezzar's wars, it represents the entire house of Israel which includes even those who were exiled by the Assyrians 130 years earlier.[337]

Ezekiel had learned that if the Lord had something in mind, something was going to happen. And that something might even be a mass restoration of the dry bones.[338] Ezekiel had been promising his people that they will be "re-membered"[339] and there will be change in their fortunes like new leadership, a restored land, rebuilt cities, and many of the features of the Messianic era.[340] If God's purpose was to restore Israel, God would do it by however great a miracle.

## 38. Can the dead bones be brought back to life?

The dead bones in the text refer to the conditions of the Babylonian exile. The gospel according to Ezekiel affirms that there is life after death, and there is hope beyond the grave.[341] With regard to HIV and AIDS, dead bones refer to the conditions that are encircled through social, economic, political, cultural and psychological setting. These dead bones can be brought back to life through the power of God. It is made possible through divine intervention.

## 39. What could have been the attitude of the prophet while prophesying to the dead bones?

There could be a dual thought in the mind of Prophet Ezekiel, i.e., on the one hand, doubt about the dead bones whether they will come alive. On the other hand, there would be intriguing daringness about the prophetical words which are revealed by God.

---

335 Daniel I. Block, *The Book of Ezekiel*, 377.

336 Katheryn Pfisterer Darr, "Ezekiel", in *The New Interpreter's Bible,* edited by Leander E Keck (Nashville: Abingdon Press, 2001), 1499.

337 Daniel I. Block, *The Book of Ezekiel*, 379.

338 Stuart Briscoe, *Dry Bones,* 123.

339 Katheryn Pfisterer Darr, "Ezekiel", 185.

340 John B. Taylor, *Ezekiel: An Introduction and Commentary,* 234.

341 Daniel I. Block, *The Book of Ezekiel*, 392.

## 40. How far does this text help you to affirm God as 'God of life'?

It is visible that the text promotes a great message that, God can create life out of nothing. This also reminds one of the creation narratives in Genesis. Mere dead bones are made to be placed in the valley, but this text guarantees that God would give life. Since God wanted to give life to the bones, flesh, breath, nerve has been provided. Initiatives are taken by God to make the dead bones alive. This ensures that in order to grant life, all the necessary things would be supplied. This helps to affirm that God as 'God of life'.

## 41. How is this story significant for AIDS affected people in India?

God did not make his prophet to stay in a royal place. The prophet was placed in a valley to prophecy and serve God. Similarly, living with HIV and AIDS is also a trouble which needs to be accepted and undergone. There is a stage of utter hopelessness in the lives of people living with HIV and AIDS. Due to the accompaniment of stigmatization, all hope is being lost.[342] Since God is a God of life, people living with HIV and AIDS need not be rejected, rather accepted in the family and society with love, care and compassion. As God performed a miracle in the prophet's time, God can do miracles in the lives of people living with HIV and AIDS. In particular, making women living with HIV and AIDS to accept themselves as they are, i.e., the very thought of hope that "I can live" is a miracle that could happen in their lives. The situation of dead bones is very pathetic when it is compared to HIV and AIDS. If God can give life to the dead bones, God could control the effect of HIV virus and prolong the life of people living with HIV and AIDS.

---

342 Dorothy BEA Akoto, "Can These Bones Live? Re-reading Ezekiel 37:1-14 in the HIV/AIDS Context," 100-101.

### 42. Does this text have any liberative elements for the AIDS sufferer? If so what are they? What lessons does the text offer to the community/church?

The Church could proclaim the message of hope using this text and invite people living with HIV and AIDS to join in the fellowship. It should motivate the suffering community to have an alternative consciousness which could affirm the very meaning and purpose of life. If God can grant life to the sufferers, there is no need to oppress and deject people living with HIV and AIDS. This text also offers a lesson to the church that it should accept the people as they are, without discriminating them.

## Conclusion

These three exegetical passages of the Hebrew Bible stand as a model for re-reading the text in the context of HIV and AIDS. The first two passages deal with skin ailments and raises issues related to stigma and discrimination. The last passage pertains to death and life which is significant in the high incidence of death that surrounds the epidemic. It argues that the theme of liberation that underpins the Hebrew Bible implies that rejection, stigma and discrimination have no place in human relations. Integration of HIV and AIDS into biblical studies could contribute towards prevention, provision of quality care, elimination of the stigma and discrimination. This exegetical study acts as an evidence for reading Biblical texts through the eyes of women living with HIV and AIDS.

Chapter 3

# Implications for the Church

## Introduction

HIV and AIDS continue to be in the forefront to cause destruction to humanity. This epidemic causes massive suffering in the lives of women living with HIV and AIDS through stigmatization and discrimination. In the previous chapter, biblical passages are interpreted through the eyes of women living with HIV and AIDS. This chapter calls for the action plan which needs to be implemented in the churches. Church needs to be committed to address the various problems of the women living with HIV and AIDS through its acceptance, care and love. It should be a sign of compassion and hope for the sufferers. This chapter gives life to the church by calling it to address the contemporary issue like HIV and AIDS.

## 1. HIV and AIDS: Is it a punishment for Sin?

The Church is considering the Bible as the authoritative written word which instructs the functioning of the church at large.[343] The OT

343 Musa W. Dube, "Grant Me Justice: Towards Gender-Sensitive Multi-sectoral HIV/AIDS Readings of the Bible", in *Grant Me Justice! HIV/AIDS & Gender*

understanding of sickness and suffering are termed as consequences of sin.[344] It is attested as, "Blessing is the reward for obedience to God and curse as reward for disobedience. Even in the present day, there is a notion that HIV and AIDS is a punishment from God and wages for sin.[345] This notion is a false assumption which needs to be tackled by the church. This false assumption is an outcome of the perspective in which the society or a particular group of people is being looked at. Women often become victims of HIV and AIDS through sexual intercourse with their husbands. For this, she cannot be branded as a sinner. It is absolutely wrong to judge her as a sinner.[346] The Church should unmask her traditional ideologies and adopt new strategies to help women living with HIV and AIDS.[347] If the theology of exclusion and condemnation is converted to a theology of inclusion and compassion, surely there would be a change in the very outlook about women living with HIV and AIDS.[348] R. L. Hnuni calls for a new hermeneutic approach to the Bible, a reading from the sufferers' perspective.[349] The Church becomes a fragmented body of Christ when she hesitates to accept women living with HIV and AIDS as a creation of God.[350] The Church cannot be an insensitive, dull and distant spectator, abandoning people to die with the curse of this

*Readings of the Bible,* edited by Musa W. Dube and Musimbi R. A. Kanyoro (South Africa: Cluster Publications, 2004), 5.

344 Kenneth R. Overberg, *Ethics and AIDS Compassion and Justice in Global Crisis* (Mumbai: St. Paul's, 2009), 4.

345 Peter Gill, *The Politics of AIDS: How They Turned a Disease into a Disaster* (New Delhi: Viva Books, 2007), 11.

346 Aravind Jayakumar, "The Church's Response to HIV/AIDS" in NCCI Review, Vol. CXXX, No. 10, Nov 2010, 602 – 603.

347 William D. Lindsey, "The AIDS Crisis and the Church: A Time to heal" in *Theology & Sexulaity – The Journal of the Institute for the Study of Christianity and Sexuality,* Edited by Elizabeth Stuart and Alison Webster, No. 2, March 1995, 12.

348 Donald E. Messer, *Breaking the Conspiracy of Silence: Christian Churches and the Global AIDS Crisis* (Delhi: ISPCK, 2007), 26.

349 Philip Kuruvilla, ed, *HIV/AIDS: A Handbook for the Church in India,* 131-132.

350 *Policy on HIV and AIDS – A Guide to Churches in India,* 5.

deadly disease. The Church cannot leave women living with HIV and AIDS in the state of hopelessness and helplessness.[351]

## 2. Bible as a Resource

Bible has become a great source to fight against the epidemic HIV and AIDS.[352] Biblical stories offer models on how to resist the challenges that are aroused due to HIV and AIDS. Experiences of women living with HIV and AIDS have similarities with the suffering experiences recorded in the Bible.[353] The Bible which is a resource for faith energizes the reader to reflect on Bible verses in the context of real life situations.[354] Even though the dominant theological thought[355] does not address HIV and AIDS explicitly, there is an alternative voice within the Bible which could be discerned in relation to suffering community. Scholars like Johanna Stiebert has already attempted to listen to this alternative voice from the perspective of HIV and AIDS. This alternative voice becomes the starting point to provide new interpretations from the perspective of the victims.[356] So, Biblical texts are opened to the re-imagination

---

351 Pramod H. Wasker, "The Church's Response to AIDS" 526.

352 Dorothy Bea Akoto, "Can These Bones Live? Re-reading Ezekiel 37:1 – 14 in the HIV/AIDS Context," in *Grant me Justice! HIV/AIDS & Gender Readings of the Bible*, edited by Musa W. Dube and Musimbi R. A. Kanyoro (South Africa: Cluster Publications, 2004), 110.

353 Musimbi R. A. Kanyoro, "Reading the Bible – in the face of HIV and AIDS," in *Grant Me Justice! HIV/AIDS & Gender Readings of the Bible,* edited by Musa W. Dube and Musimbi R.A.Kanyoro (South Africa: Cluster Publications, 2004), x-xi.

354 Monica Jyotsna Melanchthon, "Facing HIV and AIDS: Some Insights from the Hebrew Bible," in *HIV / AIDS: A Challenge to Theological Education,* edited by Samson Prabhakar & George Mathew Nalunnakkal (Bangalore: BTESSC / SATHRI, 2004), 77.

355 This thought could be the "Common Theology" of Walter Brueggemann. This theology affirms that there is a legitimated order with regard to deed and consequences.

356 Sarojini, "Barak God and Die! Women, HIV and a Theology of Suffering" in *Grant Me Justice! HIV/AIDS & Gender Readings of the Bible,* edited by Musa W. Dube and Musimbi R.A. Kanyoro (South Africa: Cluster Publications, 2004), 62-77.

from sufferers' perspective in order to obtain strength and bring hope to the wounded individual.[357] This reading with re-imagination can cause a great change in the outlook of the society towards women living with HIV and AIDS.[358]

## 3. The Task of the Church

Churches are called to heal and to be healed.[359] It is a healing[360] community which takes part in the healing ministry in the lives of women living with HIV and AIDS. HIV and AIDS is not a tragedy for the church, but it is an opportunity and challenge for the church to work with it.[361] Narrow-mindedness, insufficient knowledge and skills, denominational divisions and lack of networking among the churches and with government & NGOs have hampered the church from responding adequately to the HIV and AIDS epidemic.[362] It is the pain, stigma, exclusion, assault, lack of privacy,[363] poverty of women living with HIV and AIDS, which makes them dependent on

---

357 Letty M. Russell, "Re-Imagining the Bible in a Pandemic of HIV/AIDS" in *Grant Me Justice! HIV/AIDS & Gender Readings of the Bible,* edited by Musa W. Dube and Musimbi R.A. Kanyoro (South Africa: Cluster Publications, 2004), 201-203.

358 Musa W. Dube, "Talitha Cum! A Postcolonial Feminist & HIV/AIDS Reading of Mark 5:21-43" in *Grant Me Justice! HIV/AIDS & Gender Readings of the Bible,* edited by Musa W. Dube and Musimbi R.A. Kanyoro (South Africa: Cluster Publications, 2004), 116.

359 Musa W. Dube, *HIV and AIDS Curriculum for Theological Institutions in Africa,* (Geneva: WCC, 2001), 5.

360 Healing includes relief not only from physical sickness, but it is the healing of the whole person. William D. Lindsey, "The AIDS Crisis and the Church: A Time to heal" in *Theology & Sexulaity – The Journal of the Institute for the Study of Christianity and Sexuality,* edited by Elizabeth Stuart and Alison Webster, No. 2, March 1995, 14-15.

361 Jillian Nicholson, ed., *The Church in an HIV+ World: A Practical Handbook,* (South Africa: Cluster Publications, 2004), 39.

362 Aravind Jayakumar, "The Church's Response to HIV/AIDS" in NCCI Review, Vol. CXXX, No. 10, Nov 2010, 606-607.

363 *HIV/AIDS Training Module for Pastors & Church Workers* (Kilpauk: AIDS DESK), 39.

the welfare measures of the state and church.[364] Intimate relationship should be maintained with the women living with HIV and AIDS. This will help them to have a sense of security and they can be free from fear and anxiety.[365] The Church should be in the position to provide a climate of love, acceptance and support to them.[366] Church should act as a safe place for sharing and pouring out the cries of the sufferers.[367] Christian ethical principles like, unconditional kindness and dignity are to be affirmed to women living with HIV and AIDS.[368] Faith communities should become caring communities for the women living with HIV and AIDS by identifying themselves with the sufferers.[369] Church can stand in the gap between women living with HIV and AIDS and the resourceful people who are willing to help. Church can also act as an agent to connect the needy women with the government and non-government organizations who are willing to render services.[370]

## 4. Function of a Church Leader

The Church leader is expected to give counseling to the women living with HIV and AIDS. It is the function of the church leader to impart values and morality through preaching and interpreting the text. Preaching and teaching ministry executed in churches should educate that the women living with HIV and AIDS deserve love,

---

364 George Zechariah, "Ethics in the time of HIV and AIDS: Celebrating Infectious Memories for Positive Living" in *Asian Christian Review*, Vol. 4, No. 1, Summer 2010, 69.

365 Binita Behera, "The Doubly Disadvantaged: Widows Affected by HIV" in A Quarterly CANA Newsletter – SCAN Sentizing AIDS Action Networks, July 2010, 5.

366 WCC Document, *Facing AIDS: The Challenge, the Churches' Response* (Geneva: WCC Publications, 2000), 93.

367 WCC Document, *Facing AIDS: The Challenge, the Churches' Response*, 79.

368 Hille Haker, "A Critical Ethics of Responsibility in the Age of HIV/AIDS and Inter–Religious Dialogue" in *Negotiating Borders: Theological Explorations in the Global Era*, edited by Patrick Gnanaprasasm & Elisabeth S. Fiorenza (Delhi: ISPCK, 2008), 238.

369 Philip Kuruvilla, ed, *HIV/AIDS: A Handbook for the Church in India* (Delhi: ISPCK, 2004), 89-91.

370 Binita Behera, "The Doubly Disadvantaged: Widows Affected by HIV", 5.

compassion, along with social and emotional support.[371] They need to be embraced without any barriers, exclusion and rejection.[372] It also includes sharing of sorrow, wiping the tears, etc.[373] Church leader should lead the community to fight against Stigmatization and Discrimination.[374] It is the prime duty of the church leader to maintain strict confidentiality about the women living with HIV and AIDS.[375] It is an important responsibility of the church leader to make them feel that they are not alone. Church stands with them in their painful situation.[376]

## 5. Preaching on HIV and AIDS[377]

A pandemic like HIV and AIDS raises theological issues in the areas of creation, human nature, nature of sin and death, etc. These issues could be exposited through preaching by interpreting it in the context of HIV and AIDS.[378] Since the Bible has the potential to become a resource of encouragement and hope in the lives of women living with HIV and AIDS,[379] special time should be allotted in women's fellowship gatherings[380] to discuss about the different possibilities of interpreting the text for the empowerment of women living with HIV and AIDS. Love – Listen – Lead are the three watch

---

371 Pramod H. Wasker, "The Church's Response to AIDS" 523.

372 "AIDS and the Church as a Healing Community" in NCCI Review, Vol. CVII, No. 5, May 1987, 307-308.

373 "AIDS: A Christian View Point" in Women's Link, Vol. 2, No. 4, 1996, 60-61.

374 Philip Kuruvilla, ed, *HIV/AIDS: A Handbook for the Church in India,* 128.

375 Pramod H. Wasker, "The Church's Response to AIDS" 524.

376 Binita Behera, "The Doubly Disadvantaged: Widows Affected by HIV", 5.

377 Aravind Jayakumar, "The Church's Response to HIV/AIDS" in NCCI Review, Vol. CXXX, No. 10, Nov 2010, 608-609.

378 WCC Document, *Facing AIDS: The Challenge, the Churches' Response,* 100.

379 George Zechariah, "Ethics in the time of HIV and AIDS: Celebrating Infectious Memories for Positive Living" 79.

380 This has been humbly proposed by the researcher to be implemented in Churches.

words which could be proclaimed through Biblical interpretation in relation to women living with HIV and AIDS.[381]

## 6. Affirmation as People of God

Women are biologically,[382] epidemiologically, socially[383] vulnerable to HIV and AIDS.[384] Masenya[385] laments that because of increased vulnerability, the forces of death are currently more victorious than the forces of life.[386] They are even termed as new Dalits, outcasts and untouchables in the modern times.[387] A Theology of Creation invites everyone to call women living with HIV and AIDS as people of God. They are not sinners, but they are created by God. They are actually in need of dignity and acceptance rather than charity and sympathy.[388]

## 7. Combating Stigma/Guilt

Christian theology and Ethics condemns the stigmatization and discrimination by affirming the worth and dignity of each and

---

381 Jeya Paul Sunder Singh, "Buds of Christ" in A Quarterly CANA Newsletter – SCAN Sentizing AIDS Action Networks, July 2010, 8.

382 The rate of transmission of HIV and AIDS among women is higher than among men. In addition to the illness, women find it difficult to go for medication due to factors like stigmatization.

383 Because of husband's illegal relationships, he would have been infected with HIV and AIDS. But women do not voice their resistance to sexual relationship with the infected husband.

384 Shankar Chowdhury, "The changing AIDS Scenario: Focus on Women" in Women's Link, Vol. 2, No.4, 1996, 6-7.

385 Madipoane Masenya is the Old Testament professor at the University of South Africa.

386 Donald E. Messer, *Breaking the Conspiracy of Silence: Christian Churches and the Global AIDS Crisis,* 92.

387 George Mathew Nalunnakkal, "HIV/AIDS: Towards an Ethic of Just Care," in *HIV / AIDS: A Challenge to Theological Education,* edited by Samson Prabhakar & George Mathew Nalunnakkal (Bangalore: BTESSC / SATHRI, 2004), 22-23.

388 Erlind N. Senturias, "God's Mission and HIV/AIDS: Shaping the Churches' Response" in International Review of Mission, Vol. LXXXIII, No. 329, 1994, 277-278.

every individual as being created by God.[389] Church should be in the forefront to fight against any advances that alienate, isolate and discriminate women living with HIV and AIDS. Stigma kills more than HIV itself. Kalpana Jain is of the opinion that women living with HIV and AIDS have more fear about the stigma and shame they face, than the fear of early death.[390] Stigma forces women to hesitate and seek counseling and medication. If the church remains silent, then invariably the church is in the process of perpetuating stigma and discrimination.[391] Refusal of Holy Communion and decent funerals are also part of discrimination which needs to be bunged,[392] because it intensifies the trauma of suffering.[393] Welcoming and considering women living with HIV and AIDS as a valuable resource, breaking the conspiracy of silence, encouraging theological and ethical reflection on HIV and AIDS could be adopted by the church to combat stigma.[394] Their experiences would also contribute to strengthen the commitment of the churches and communities.[395] But at any cost, women living with HIV and AIDS and their experiences should not be looked as an object of study.[396]

389 Donald E. Messer, *Breaking the Conspiracy of Silence: Christian Churches and the Global AIDS Crisis,* 63.

390 Kalpana Jain, *Positive Lives: The Story of Ashok and others with HIV* (New Delhi: Penguin Publications, 2002), 20.

391 *Policy on HIV and AIDS – A Guide to Churches in India,* (Nagpur: NCCI/ ISPCK, 2009), 6.

392 John S. Sadananda, "HIV/AIDS: A Challenge to Theological Education and Some Possible Responses" in *HIV / AIDS: A Challenge to Theological Education,* 105.

393 Donald E. Messer, *Breaking the Conspiracy of Silence: Christian Churches and the Global AIDS Crisis,* 60.

394 Aravind Jayakumar, "The Church's Response to HIV/AIDS" in NCCI Review, Vol. CXXX, No. 10, Nov 2010, 607-608.

395 A. Wati Longchar, "HIV/AIDS: A Challenge to Theological Education in Asia" in *HIV/AIDS: A Challenge to Theological Education,* 120.

396 Samson Prabhakar, "A Brief Report on the Consultation" in *HIV/AIDS: A Challenge to Theological Education,* 133.

As a practical implication, in order to wrestle against stigma, an anti-stigma campaign could be organized.[397]

## 8. Advocacy

Advocacy is one of the ways through which an individual can exhibit love and care to the women living with HIV and AIDS.[398] Church has the positive impact in changing the psychology of the women living with HIV and AIDS. When the church embraces women living with HIV and AIDS, they experience love, compassion and support.[399] The outcome of Koinonia could occur in the lives of women living with HIV and AIDS.[400] In the church scenario, koinonia could be practiced by sitting and eating with the women living HIV and AIDS.[401] But when stigma and discrimination are employed, the very essence of the value of Koinonia is lost.[402]

## 9. Attitudinal Change

Human suffering is not an occasion for the church to make external judgments or to debate as to whom or what the cause of suffering is. Instead, the church should offer unconditional care and compassion. By this, individuals, families and communities become responsive to exhibit and affirm mutual love with the suffering community. It is such an empowered community that will live in fellowship with rejected and stigmatized women living with HIV and AIDS,

---

397 Arvind Singhal & Everett M. Rogers, *Combating AIDS: Communication Strategies in Action* (New Delhi: Sage Publications, 2003), 252.

398 *Grace, Care and Justice - A Handbook for HIV and AIDS Work,* (Geneva: Lutheran World Federation, 2007), 88.

399 Aravind Jayakumar, "The Church's Response to HIV/AIDS" in NCCI Review, Vol. CXXX, No. 10, Nov 2010, 608.

400 Erlind N. Senturias, "God's Mission and HIV/AIDS: Shaping the Churches' Response, 283-284.

401 David Augustine, "HIV/AIDS" in *Gurukul Daily Devotion* Nov 6, 2007, edited by Suneel Bhanu (Kilpauk: Gurukul Lutheran Theological College, 2007), 355.

402 Donald E. Messer, *Breaking the Conspiracy of Silence: Christian Churches and the Global AIDS Crisis,* 21.

without prejudge and judgment.[403] The Church should work as a redeeming community to redeem women living with HIV and AIDS into a state of acceptance (being inclusive) and not rejection. For W. E. Amos, "inclusiveness is a way of being, living, working and worshipping together."[404] Church should not try to find out how a person received HIV and AIDS.[405] There is a need that there should not be any behavior with prejudices or preconceived notions. Words of judgment and condemnation are to be totally avoided with a call to behavioral and attitudinal change.[406]

## 10. Action plan

The Church can conduct AIDS awareness programs through seminars and workshops.[407] Special programs and services could be conducted to meet the needs of women living with HIV and AIDS and also the needs of family members.[408] Even though, some activities are initiated for the prevention and care of HIV and AIDS, it is inhibited through socio-cultural norms and stereotypes.[409] Topics related to sexual health, sexuality, abstinence should be discussed openly in churches. In order to prevent the spread of HIV, discussion needs to be done publicly about sex. Education could act as a most effective weapon against HIV.[410] Along with sex education, health facilities and health education, legal support and rehabilitation needs to be given for the social and economic empowerment of women living with HIV and

403 *Policy on HIV and AIDS – A Guide to Churches in India* (Nagpur: NCCI/ISPCK, 2009), 5.

404 William E. Amos, *When AIDS Come to Church* (Philadelphia: Westminster John Knox Press, 1940), 17.

405 Pramod H. Wasker, "The Church's Response to AIDS" 524-525.

406 Norman Noah, *Controlling Communicable Disease* (New Delhi: Tata McGraw Hill Publishing Company Limited, 2006), 223.

407 Pramod H. Wasker, "The Church's Response to AIDS" in National Council of Churches Review, Vol. CXV, No. 6, 1995, 521-523.

408 Philip Kuruvilla, ed, *HIV/AIDS: A Handbook for the Church in India,* 122.

409 Radhika Ramasubban, "HIV/AIDS in India – Gulf between Rhetoric and Reality" in *Economic and Political Weekly*, Vol. XXXIII, No. 45, 1998, 2872.

410 Pernessa C. Seele, "The Church's Role in HIV/AIDS Prevention" in *Anglican Theological Review*, Vol. 77, No.4, 1995, 550-551.

AIDS.[411] Special efforts could be made among women's groups to be well aware of the legal rights, counseling, testing services, etc. Women living with HIV and AIDS need to be involved in decision making with regard to policy and welfare measures.[412] Since there is a dramatic advancement in the field of computer and technology, church can propagate positive message about women living with HIV and AIDS through its innovative programs.[413]

## 11. Expectations of Women Living with HIV and AIDS

Women suffering from HIV and AIDS request that we reach out personally and listen to the stories of women living with HIV and AIDS. By the very sharing of the troubles, there would be relief in their hearts and minds. Extending financial, spiritual and moral support to the women living with HIV and AIDS is the need of the hour. They seek empathy while dealing with emotions and request that we do not make judgmental statements, stigmatize them and reject them, but that we accept them with love.

## Conclusion

The Churches should be in a position to accept the challenges caused by HIV and AIDS. In the present hour, offering courage, hope, support to the women living with HIV and AIDS is the noteworthy responsibility of the church. There should not be any involvement of the faith communities to pass judgmental comments about women living with HIV and AIDS. This chapter calls for reimaging biblical stories to seek reflections in favour of women living with HIV and AIDS which is to be implemented in churches.

---

411 Atanu Sarkar, "AIDS/HIV Infection and Victimization of Women" in *Women's Link*, Vol. 2, No. 4, 1996, 4.

412 Shankar Chowdhury, "The Changing AIDS Scenario: Focus on Women" in *Women's Link*, Vol. 2, No. 4, 1996, 9.

413 Shankar Chowdhury, "The Changing AIDS Scenario: Focus on Women" in *Women's Link*, 8.

# Conclusion

This research work reveals the danger of HIV and AIDS along with the process of conversion from HIV to AIDS. Effects on social, economic, cultural, psychological and religious aspects of life due to HIV and AIDS expose the reality of the suffering community. Stigma, discrimination and rejection of the sufferer affect the relationships within family and also in work spot. In the research, notable importance is being given to women who are living with HIV and AIDS. Inequalities based on gender, violence against women, medical differences makes women living with HIV and AIDS more vulnerable in the society. In the process of accommodating HIV positive women in the society, legislation should offer non-discrimination and encourage community participation. Protective nature of the law offers protection against discrimination & stigmatization and potential nature of the law revisits the socio-economic patterns of the pandemic. Even though, Hebrew Bible does not explicitly deal with HIV and AIDS, sicknesses and diseases run through the Bible. Basically, there are many theological questions being raised about the presence of God in the midst of suffering. In the case of HIV and AIDS, sufferers are blamed as sinners. But in many cases women become vulnerable by being infected by their husbands. Bible is not meant to be used for making moral judgments alone. But it needs to be used as a liberative tool for the many sufferers by re-reading and re-imaging the Bible from the sufferers' perspective.

In order to provide quality care and to eliminate stigma and discrimination, bible stories about sicknesses could be re-interpreted from the perspective of women living with HIV and AIDS. So that Bible becomes meaningful in their lives. This becomes an agent of hope and words of encouragement in the midst of suffering. Using the reader's response methodology, traditional understandings of blame placed on Miriam in Numbers 12:10-16 is being unmasked. Reading from women's perspective, the study reveals that Miriam slandered as a protest to the marriage of Cushite woman by Moses. This rebellion has been made by Miriam due to the doubt that Moses would move away from Yahweh. According to the Midrash, she was a role model. She was an advocate of the Biblical command to 'be fruitful and multiply'. Furthermore, it is nothing wrong to ask the question whether God speaks only through Moses. Because, there were seventy leaders being appointed upon whom God's spirit descended. They were appointed during the people's rebellion for the dissatisfaction about 'Manna" - the daily food. Even though, Miriam was struck with leprosy, the very act of waiting by the community until the restoration of Miriam's health reminds the reader that she was a skilled leader. This story condemns the act of branding women living with HIV and AIDS as sinners. There cannot be any blaming of the women living with HIV and AIDS for their suffering. The act of excommunicating women living with HIV and AIDS invites critique citing Miriam's experience.

2 Kings 5:8 – 14 is about Naaman's skin ailment and healing at Jordan River. Even though, there is no mention about the name of the wife of Naaman and the Hebrew slave girl, they played a significant role in the process of healing. Naaman was not gifted a red carpet treatment by the prophet. Instead, he was asked to wash in Jordan River seven times. This statement of the prophet kindled the anger of Naaman. But it was re-echoed by his servants calling Naaman to obey. Exposition of Physical, psychological, social and religious imaginations and sufferings of Naaman, gives the message of courage to women living with HIV and AIDS. Naaman was not free from shame and illness even though he was holding a respectful position in Syria. His position made him not to be deserted from the society.

But the frustration and humiliation due to the sickness would have existed. The same frustration, inferiority complex, shame, hurdles in work spot, etc., are the present experiences of the women living with HIV and AIDS. When these stories of suffering are read from the Bible with heart and mind, it gives space to relate oneself with the sufferers which might give some kind of consolation to the readers.

Ezekiel 37:1-14 speaks about the death and life in which the message of hope is retrieved for the reader. Here, the prophet Ezekiel does not function as a mere observer but as an active participant in carrying out God's mission. He was an agent in bringing life to the dry bones. Divine voice is being heard by the prophet and he responded positively. This passage also gives a practical implication that since God is a God of life, women living with HIV and AIDS need not be rejected, rather accepted in the family and society with love, care and compassion. It motivates the suffering community to have an alternative consciousness which could affirm the very meaning and purpose of life. The very thought of hope that "I can live" is a miracle that could happen in their lives. It gives the message of hope to the suffering community. This text also makes women living with HIV and AIDS to accept themselves as they are. This text also offers a lesson to the church that it should accept the people as they are, without discriminating them.

These three exegetical passages stand as samples to affirm that Biblical texts could be used to address the multifaceted illness which are prevailing in the contemporary world. Bible is not an isolated book. It speaks to its readers by sharing the message of hope and encouragement. It also helps to retrieve messages for practical life.

In the journey of research, the study also reveals some implications for the church. HIV and AIDS should no more be looked as a wage for sin. It is a challenge for the humanity to tackle the illness like HIV and AIDS in this present day. In the midst of suffering, church should play a key role to fight against discrimination, stigmatization, rejection, etc. This could be done by keeping Bible as a source of inspiration and by interpreting the text from reader's perspective. Biblical interpretations should strive to consider women living with

HIV and AIDS as people of God. This would also enhance women living with HIV and AIDS to consider themselves as worth living. Preaching could also bring attitudinal change about the sufferers. Therefore, the Hebrew Bible could be used to combat major issues like HIV and AIDS in the present society.

# Appendix - A

### Numbers 12:10-16

- Why was Miriam being punished with leprosy?
- What sort of pain would Miriam have experienced when she was infected with leprosy?
- What in your imaginations was Miriam's feeling when she was placed outside the camp?
- How is this story significant for AIDS affected people in India?
- Does this text have any liberative elements for the AIDS sufferer? If so what are they? What lessons does the text offer to the community/church?

### 2 Kings 5:8-14

- Why was Naaman seeking to have his leprosy cured?
- What were Naaman's expectations when he was washing himself in the Jordan River?
- Since Naaman was infected with leprosy, what problems might he have faced as a captain for the army of King Syria?
- How is this story significant for AIDS affected people in India?
- Does this text have any liberative elements for the AIDS sufferer? If so what are they? What lessons does the text offer to the community/church?

## Ezekiel 37:1-14

- Can the dead bones be brought back to life?
- What could have been the attitude of the prophet while prophesying to the dead bones?
- How far does this text help you to affirm God as 'God of life'?
- How is this story significant for AIDS affected people in India?
- Does this text have any liberative elements for the AIDS sufferer? If so what are they? What lessons does the text offer to the community/church?

## General Questions:

- How is the skin ailment (leprosy), comparable to AIDS?
- Explain about stigma, discrimination and rejection faced by you (woman living with AIDS)?
- What are your expectations from the church?
- What do you anticipate from the church leader/pastor?
- What do you look forward to from the church congregational members?

# Appendix - B

எண்ணாகமம் 12:10-16

- மிரியாம் ஏன் தொழுநோயினால் (Leprosy) தண்டிக்கப்பட்டாள்?
- மிரியாம் தொழுநோயினால் (Leprosy) பாதிக்கப்பட்ட நேரத்தில் எவ்விதமான வலி வேதனைகளை அனுபவித்திருப்பாள்?
- மிரியாம் பாளயத்திற்கு வெளியே இருக்க செய்த சமயத்தில், அவளுடைய மனநிலை எப்படி இருந்திருக்கும் என்று நீங்கள் சிந்திக்கிறீர்கள்?
- இந்த கதை இந்தியாவிலுள்ள AIDS நோயால் பாதிக்கபட்டவர்களுக்கு எந்த விதத்தில் பொருளுடையதாயிருக்கும்?
- இந்த வேதபகுதியில் AIDS நோயால் பாதிக்கபட்டவர்களுக்கு ஏதாகிலும் சத்தியங்கள் உண்டா? ஆம் என்றால், என்ன பாடத்தை இந்த வேதபகுதி திருச்சபைக்கும், சமுதாயத்திற்கும் கற்றுகொடுக்கிறது?

2 இராஜாக்கள் 5:8-14

- நாகமான் ஏன் தன் குஷ்டரோகம் குணமாக வேண்டுமென்று விரும்பினான்?
- யோர்தான் நதியிலே நாகமான் ஸ்நானம் பன்னினபோது

அவனுடைய மனநிலையிலே எப்படிப்பட்ட எதிர்பார்புகள் இருந்திருக்கும்?

- நாகமான் குஷ்டரோகியாய் இருந்தபடியினால், சீரியா இராஜாவின் படை தலைவனாய் எப்படிப்பட்ட பிரச்சனைகளை சந்தித்திருப்பான்?
- இந்த கதை இந்தியாவிலுள்ள AIDS நோயால் பாதிக்கபட்டவர்களுக்கு எந்த விதத்தில் பொருளுடையதாயிருக்கும்?
- இந்த வேதபகுதியில் AIDS நோயால் பாதிக்கபட்டவர்களுக்கு ஏதாகிலும் சத்தியங்கள் உண்டா? ஆம் என்றால், என்ன பாடத்தை இந்த வேதபகுதி திருச்சபைக்கும், சமுதாயத்திற்கும் கற்றுகொடுக்கிறது?

எசேக்கியேல் 37:1-14

- உலர்ந்த எலும்புகள் உயிர்பெறுமா?
- உலர்ந்த எலும்புகளை பார்த்து தீர்க்கதரிசனம் உரைக்கும்போது, தீர்க்கதரிசியின் எண்ணம் எப்படி இருந்திருக்கும்?
- "தேவன் ஜீவன் அளிப்பவர்" என்பதை அறிக்கையிட இந்த வசனங்கள் எவ்வாறு உதவுகிறது?
- இந்த கதை இந்தியாவிலுள்ள AIDS நோயால் பாதிக்கபட்டவர்களுக்கு எந்த விதத்தில் பொருளுடையதாயிருக்கும்?
- இந்த வேதபகுதியில் AIDS நோயால் பாதிக்கபட்டவர்களுக்கு ஏதாகிலும் சத்தியங்கள் உண்டா? ஆம் என்றால், என்ன பாடத்தை இந்த வேதபகுதி திருச்சபைக்கும், சமுதாயத்திற்கும் கற்றுகொடுக்கிறது?

பொதுவான கேள்விகள்

- தொழுநோய் (Leprosy) வியாதியை AIDS யோடு எப்படி ஒப்பிடுவது?
- உங்கள் வாழ்கையில் நீங்கள் சந்திந்த ஒடுக்குதலை பற்றி சொல்ல முடியுமா?
- திருச்சபையிடமிருந்து நீங்கள் எதிர்பார்க்கின்ற காரியங்கள் என்ன?

- திருச்சபை தலைவர்கள் / போதகர்களிடமிருந்து நீங்கள் எதிர்பார்க்கின்ற காரியங்கள் என்ன?
- திருச்சபை விசுவாசிகளிடமிருந்து நீங்கள் எதிர்ப்பார்க்கின்ற காரியங்கள் என்ன?

# Bibliography


## Bibles and Lexicons

*Biblia Hebraica Stuttgartensia.* Germany: Deutsche Bibelgellschaft, 1997.

*New Revised Standard Version.* Michigan: Zondervan Bible Publishers, 1990.

*Revised Standard Version.* Second edition. Nashville: Thomas Nelson Publishers, 1983.

Brown, F., S. Driver and C. Briggs. *The Brown Driver Briggs Hebrew and English Lexicon.* USA: Hendirckson Publishers, 2001.

## Dictionaries and Commentaries

Budd, Philip J. *Numbers.* WBC. *Vol. 5.* Dallas, Texas: Word Books Publisher, 1998.

Buttrick, George Arthur. *The Interpreter's Bible.* Vol. 3. Nashville: Abingdon Press, 1954.

Clements, Roland E. *1 and 2 Kings.* New Century Bible Commentary. London: Eerdmans Publishing, 1984.

Eichrodt, Walther. *Ezekiel: A Commentary.* Philadelphia: The Westminster John Knox Press, 1970.

Gray, John. *I & II Kings: A Commentary.* London: SCM Press Ltd, 1964.

Harrison, R.K. and Robert L Hubbard. Eds. *The Book of Ezekiel.* NICOT. Michigan: Eerdmans, 1998.

Hobbs, R. T. *2 Kings.* WBC. Vol. 13. Texas: Word Books Publisher, 1985.

Hubbard, David A. & Glenn W. Baker. Eds. *Ezekiel 20-48.* WBC. Vol. 29. Texas: Word Books Publisher, 1990.

Keck, Leander E. Ed. *The New Interpreter's Bible.* Nashville: Abingdon Press, 2001.

Laffery, Alice L. *First Kings and Second Kings: Collegeville Bible Commentary.* Mumbai: St. Paul's, 2001.

Montgomery, James A. *A Critical and Exegetical Commentary on the Books of Kings.* Edinburgh: T & T Clark, 1976.

Nelson, Richard D. *First and Second Kings: Interpretation – A Bible Commentary for Teaching and Preaching.* Atlanta: Westminster John Knox Press, 1987.

Newson, Carol A. & Sharon H. Ringe. Eds. *The Women's Bible Commentary.* Louisville: John Knox Press, 1992.

Noth, Martin. *Numbers – A Commentary.* London: SCM Press, 1968.

Robinson, J. *The Second Book of Kings.* CBC. New York: Cambridge University Press, 1987.

Taylor, John B. *Ezekiel: An Introduction and Commentary.* Leicester: Inter-Varsity Press, 1969.

Wenham, Gordon J. *Numbers: An Introduction and Commentary.* Illinois: Inter-Varsity Press, 1981.

Wiseman, Donald J. *1 and 2 Kings.* Tyndale Old Testament Commentaries London: Inter-Varsity Press, 1993.

Zimmerli, W. *Ezekiel 2: A Commentary on the Book of the Prophet Ezekiel.* Philadelphia: Fortress Press, 1983.

## Encyclopedia

Satpathy, G. C. *Encyclopedia of AIDS.* Vol. 3. Delhi: Kalpaz Publications, 2003.

## Monographs

Amos, William E. *When AIDS Come to Church.* Philadelphia: Westminster John Knox Press, 1940.

Auld, Graeme. *I & II Kings.* Philadelphia: Westminster John Knox Press, 1986.

Becking, Bob & Meindert Dijkstra. *On Reading Prophetic Texts: Gender-Specific and Related Studies in Memory of Fokkelien van Dijk-Hemmes.* New York: E.J. Brill, 1996.

Bergen, Wesley J. *Elisha and the End of Prophetism.* England: Sheffield Academic Press, 1999.

Bhanu, Suneel. Ed. *Gurukul Daily Devotion.* Kilpauk: Gurukul Lutheran Theological College, 2007.

Binns, Elliott. *The Book of Numbers.* London: Methuen & Co Ltd, 1927.

Blackwood, Andrew W. *Ezekiel: Prophecy of Hope.* Michigan: Bakers Book House, 1965.

Block, Daniel I. *The Book of Ezekiel: Chapters 25-48.* Michigan: Eerdmans, 1997.

Brenner, Athalya. Ed. *Feminist Companion to Exodus to Deuteronomy.* England: Sheffield Academic Press, 1994.

________, *The Israelite Woman: Social Role and Literary Type in Biblical Narrative.* England: JSOT Press, 1985.

________, *Samuel and Kings: A The Feminist Companion to the Bible.* England: Sheffield Academic Press, 2000.

________, *A Feminist Companion to Samuel and Kings.* England: Sheffield Academic Press, 1994.

Briscoe, Stuart. *Dry Bones.* USA: Victor Books, 1977.

Cogan, Mordechai. & Hayim Tadmor. *2 Kings.* USA: Doubleday & Company, 1988.

Cook, Rebecca J. *Human Rights of Women: National and International Perspectives.* Philadelphia: Pennsylvania Press, 1994.

Cooke, G. A. *The Book of Ezekiel.* Edinburgh: T & T Clark, 1951.

Das, Somen. *Woman in India.* Calcutta: ISPCK, 1997.

Day, Peggy L. *Gender and Difference in Ancient Israel.* Minneapolis: Fortress Press, 1989.

Deen, Edith. *All of the Women of the Bible.* San Francisco: Harper & Row Publication, 1983.

Dentan, R. C. *I & II Kings, I & II Chronicles.* London: SCM Press Ltd, 1964.

Dube, Musa W. *HIV and AIDS Curriculum for Theological Institutions in Africa.* Geneva: WCC, 2001.

Dube, Musa W. Ed. *HIV/AIDS and the Curriculum: Methods of Integrating HIV/AIDS in Theological Programmes.* Geneva: WCC Publications, 2003.

________, & Musimbi R. A. Kanyoro. Eds. *Grant me Justice! HIV/AIDS & Gender Readings of the Bible.* South Africa: Cluster publications, 2004.

Ellison, H. L. *Ezekiel: The Man and His Message.* Michigan: Eerdmans, 1956.

Facilitator's Guide. *Prescriptions for Hope.* USA: Samaritan's Purse, 2005.

Faden, Ruth R. & Nancy E. Kass. Eds. *HIV/AIDS and Childbearing: Public Policy, Private Lives.* New York: Oxford University Press, 1996.

Gennrich, Daniela. *The Church in an HIV+ World: A Practical Handbook.* South Africa: Cluster Publications, 2004.

Gill, Deborah M. and Barbara Cavaness. *God's Women: Then and Now.* Secunderabad: Authentic Media, 2007.

Gill, Peter. *The Politics of AIDS: How They Turned a Disease into a Disaster.* New Delhi: Viva Books, 2007.

Gnanaprasasm, Patrick. & Elisabeth S. Fiorenza. *Negotiating Borders: Theological Explorations in the Global Era.* Delhi: ISPCK, 2008.

Gothoskar, Sujatha. *Struggles of Women at Work.* New Delhi: Vikas Publishing House Pvt. Ltd, 1992.

*Grace, Care and Justice - A Handbook for HIV and AIDS Work.* Geneva: Lutheran World Federation, 2007.

Howarth, Henriette. *The Breaking of Her Dawn: Six Bible Studies from the Old Testament.* Hyderabad: YWCA, 2000.

Hurley, James B. *Man and Woman in Biblical Perspective: A Study in Role Relationships and Authority.* England: InterVarsity Press, 1981.

*Institute of Medicine and the National Academy of Sciences: Confronting AIDS.* Washington DC: National Academy Press, 1989.

Irene Nowell OSB, *Women in the Old Testament.* Minnesota: Liturgical Press, 1997.

Jain, Kalpana. *Positive Lives: The Story of Ashok and others with HIV.* New Delhi: Penguin Publications, 2002.

Jayasuriya, D. C. Ed. *HIV: Law, Ethics and Human Rights,* New Delhi: UNDP, 1995.

Kuruvilla, Philip. Ed. *HIV/AIDS: A Handbook for the Church in India.* Delhi: ISPCK, 2004.

Kuyper, Abraham. *Women of the Old Testament.* Michigan: Zondervan Publishing House, 1976.

Laffey, Alice L. *An Introduction to the Old Testament: A Feminist Perspective.* Philadelphia: Fortress Press, 1988.

Lockyer, Herbert. *The Women of the Bible.* Michigan: Zondervan Publishing House, 1967.

Long, Burke O. *2 Kings.* Michigan: William B. Eerdmans Publishing Company, 1991.

Lundholm, Theodor Algot. *Women of the Bible.* Illinois: Augustana Book Concern, 1948.

Matthews, Victor H., Bernard M. Levinson and Tikva Frymer-Kensky. *Gender and Law in the Hebrew Bible and the Ancient Near East.* England: Sheffield Academic Press Ltd, 1998.

Melanchthon, Monica J. *Rejection by God: The History and Significance of the Rejection Motif in the Hebrew Bible.* New York: Peter Lang Publishing Inc, 2001.

Messer, Donald E. *Breaking the Conspiracy of Silence: Christian Churches and the Global AIDS Crisis.* Delhi: ISPCK, 2007.

Misra, Lakshmi. *Women's Issues: An Indian Perspective.* New Delhi: Northern Book Centre, 1992.

Nicholson, Jillian. Ed. *The Church in an HIV+ World: A Practical Handbook.* South Africa: Cluster Publications, 2004.

Noah, Norman. *Controlling Communicable Disease.* New Delhi: Tata McGraw Hill Publishing Company Limited, 2006.

Noth, Martin. *Exodus.* London: SCM Press, 1962.

Oesterley, E. & Theodore H. *An Introduction to the Books of the Old Testament.* London: Macmillan Company, 1949.

Overberg, Kenneth R. *Ethics & AIDS: Compassion and Justice in Global Crisis.* Mumbai: St. Pauls Press, 2009.

Panda, Samiran, Anindya Chatterjee, and Abu S. Abdul-Queder. *Living with AIDS Virus: The Epidemic and the Response in India.* New Delhi: SAGE Publications, 2002.

*Policy on HIV and AIDS – A Guide to Churches in India.* Nagpur: NCCI/ISPCK, 2009.

Prabhakar, Samson & George Mathew Nalunnakkal, eds. *HIV/AIDS: A Challenge to Theological Education.* Bangalore: BTESSC / SATHRI, 2004.

Premkumar, Daniel. *Ronnie's Bible.* Kilpauk: AIDS DESK, 2007.

Rad, Gerhard von. "Naaman: A Critical Retelling" in *God at Work in Israel.* Nashville: Abingdon Press, 1980.

Ramaiah, Savitri. *HIV and AIDS.* New Delhi: Sterling Publishers, 2008.

Robinson, Theodore H. *The Decline and Fall of the Hebrew Kingdoms.* Oxford: Clarendon Press, 1952.

Sahu, Sathyarthi & Sarah, Sahu. *Counsel for Crisis Times.* Delhi: Cambridge Press, 2009.

Singhal, Arvind & Everett M. Rogers. *Combating AIDS: Communication Strategies in Action.* New Delhi: Sage Publications, 2003.

Smith, George Adam. *Historical Geography of the Holy Land.* London: Hodder & Stoughton, 1931.

Snaith, N. H. *Leviticus and Numbers.* London: Thomas Nelson Printers, 1967.

Stanton, Elizabeth Cady. *The Woman's Bible.* Seattle: Task force on Women and Religion, 1974.

Thomas, Gracious. *AIDS in India.* New Delhi: Rawat Publications, 1994.

Timothy, Ashley R. *The Book of Numbers.* Michigan: Eerdmans , 1993.

Trible, Phyllis. *Texts of Terror.* Philadelphia: Fortress Press, 1984.

Wallace, Ronald S. *Elijah and Elisha: Expositions from the Book of Kings.* Edinburgh: Oliver and Boyd, 1957.

Walter, Kaiser C. *Toward Old Testament Ethics.* Michigan: Zondervan Publishing House, 1983.

Wenham, Gordon J. *Numbers.* England: Sheffield Academic Press, 1997.

Wevers, John W. Ed. *Ezekiel.* London: Thomas Nelson and Sons Ltd., 1969.

Whybray, R. N. *Ezekiel.* England: JSOT Press, 1993.

Wold, Margaret. *Women of Faith & Spirit: Profiles of Fifteen Biblical Witnesses.* Minneapolis: Augsburg Publishing House, 1987.

WCC Study Document. *Facing AIDS: The Challenge, the Church's Response.* Geneva: WCC Publications, 1997.

## Journals

Behera, Binita. "The Doubly Disadvantaged: Widows Affected by HIV." *A Quarterly CANA Newsletter – SCAN Sentizing AIDS Action Networks,* (July 2010) 1-28.

Chowdhury, Shankar. "The changing AIDS Scenario: Focus on Women." *Women's Link.* Vol. 2, No.4 (1996) 5-9.

Levine, Bayer R. & Walf S. M. "HIV antibody screening: an ethical framework for evaluating proposed programs." *Journal of American Medical Association* (1986) 64-68.

Ramasubban, Radhika. "HIV/AIDS in India – Gulf between Rhetoric and Reality." *Economic and Political Weekly.* Vol. XXXIII, No. 45 (1998) 2865-2872.

Stuart, Elizabeth & Alison Webster. Eds. *Theology & Sexuality – The Journal of the Institute for the Study of Christianity and Sexuality.* No. 2 (March, 1995) 11-37.

## Reviews

"AIDS and the Church as a Healing Community." *NCCI Review.* Vol. CVII, No. 5 (May, 1987), 307-308.

"AIDS: A Christian View Point." *Women's Link.* Vol. 2, No. 4 (1996), 60-61.

Jayakumar, Aravind. "The Church's Response to HIV/AIDS" *NCCI Review.* Vol. CXXX, No. 10 (Nov. 2010), 49-60.

Lai, Ngan Elizabeth Ling. "2 Kings 5." *Review and Expositor*. Vol. 94, No. 4 (1997), 589-598.

Sarkar, Atanu. "AIDS/HIV Infection and Victimization of Women." *Women's Link*. Vol. 2, No. 4 (1996), 2-4.

Seele, Pernessa C. "The Church's Role in HIV/AIDS Prevention." *Anglican Theological Review*. Vol. 77, No. 4 (1995), 550-551.

Senturias, Erlind N. "God's Mission and HIV/AIDS: Shaping the Churches' Response." *International Review of Mission*. Vol. LXXXIII, No. 329 (1994), 277-284.

Wasker, Pramod H. "The Church's Response to AIDS." *National Council of Churches Review*. Vol. CXV, No. 6 (1995), 521-523.

Zechariah, George. "Ethics in the time of HIV and AIDS: Celebrating Infectious Memories for Positive Living." *Asian Christian Review*. Vol. 4, No. 1 (Summer, 2010), 67-81.

## Electronic Sources

http://www.wen.org.uk/gen_eng/Genetics/tampon1.htm (2.10.2010 7pm)

http://www.tibotechiv.com/gldisplay.jhtml?itemname=glossary#gl_Antiretroviralmedications (28.9.2010 5pm)

http://www.suite101.com/content/treatment-for-hivaids-a54642 (29.9.2010 12pm)

http://www.medicinenet.com/swollen_lymph_nodes/symptoms.htm(4.10.2010 2.30pm)

http://www.fao.org/docrep/x0259e/x0259e02.htm#TopOfPage (4.10.2010 4.30pm)

http://www.dosomething.org/actnow/tipsandtools/the-effect-hivaids-society (4.10.2010 6pm)

http://www.ehow.com/facts_5144656_social-effect-hiv-aids.html (25.10.2010 3pm)

http://www.ipu.org/PDF/publications/aids_en.pdf (26.10.2010 3pm)

http://www.undp.org/hiv/publications/issues/english/issue11e.htm#The%20protective%20role%20of%20law (26/10/2010 10:45pm) http://www.un.org/apps/news/story.asp?NewsID=34977&Cr=aids&Cr1 (27/10/2010 12:30pm)

http://www.who.int/hiv/topics/prophylaxis/en/ (10/1/2011 8:00pm)

http://www.who.int/hiv/topics/microbicides/microbicides/en/ (10/1/2011 8:30pm)

http://www.aidsinfo.nih.gov/DrugsNew/DrugDetailNT.aspx?int_id=116 (3/11/2010 8am)

http://www.britannica.com/EBchecked/topic/46868/AZT (3/11/2010 11am)

http://www.whereincity.com/medical/topic/women-health/diseases/pelvic-inflammatory-disease-10.htm (4/11/2010 10.30pm)

http://www.nlm.nih.gov/medlineplus/ency/article/002317.htm (4/11/2010 11.15pm)

http://www.medicinenet.com/premenstrual_syndrome/article.htm (4/11/2010 11.50pm)

http://journals.lww.com/jaids/Abstract/2009/08150/Intimate_Partner_Violence_Functions_as_Both_a_Risk.13.aspx (6/11/2010 11.15am)

http://www.amnestyusa.org/women/rapeinwartime.html (6/11/2010 11.35am)

http://www.avert.org/women-hiv-aids.htm (8/11/2010 01:02 pm)

http://www.hastingswomenslj.org/ (15/11/2010 11am)